Untapped
MAGIC

Untapped
MAGIC

Manifestation Methods
for Living a *Limitless Life*

CHLOE PANTA

New World Library
Novato, California

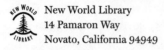

New World Library
14 Pamaron Way
Novato, California 94949

Text design by Tona Pearce Myers

Library of Congress Cataloging-in-Publication Data

Names: Panta, Chloe, author.
Title: Untapped magic : manifestation methods for living a limitless life / Chloe
   Panta.
Description: Novato, California : New World Library, [2024] | Summary: "In
   Untapped Magic, life coach and entrepreneur Chloe Panta shares her per-
   sonal journey from growing up in poverty in Detroit to creating a successful
   career and life. She offers readers practical advice on how to tap into their
   own inner magic and create the life they desire"-- Provided by publisher.
Identifiers: LCCN 2023053643 (print) | LCCN 2023053644 (ebook) |
   ISBN 9781608688906 (paperback) | ISBN 9781608688913 (epub)
Subjects: LCSH: Self-realization. | Spirituality.
Classification: LCC BF637.S4 P3474 2024 (print) | LCC BF637.S4 (ebook) |
   DDC 158.1--dc23/eng/20231218
LC record available at https://lccn.loc.gov/2023053643
LC ebook record available at https://lccn.loc.gov/2023053644

First printing, March 2024
ISBN 978-1-60868-890-6
Ebook ISBN 978-1-60868-891-3
Printed in Canada on 100% postconsumer-waste recycled paper

New World Library is proud to be a Gold Certified Environmentally Responsible Publisher. Publisher certification awarded by Green Press Initiative.

10   9   8   7   6   5   4   3   2   1

To 2004 Chloe. You did it, girl. You did it.

Let nothing dim the light that shines from within.

— MAYA ANGELOU

Contents

Part 4: Change Your Mind
to Change Your Reality

Introduction

*Difficulties in your life did not come to destroy you
but to help you realize your hidden potential and power.
Let difficulties know that you too are difficult.*

— A. P. J. ABDUL KALAM, Atomic Scientist,
President of India, Overcomer of Obstacles

I'm assuming that if you're here, you're looking for some way
out of something. You're looking for a magical pill or potion
to make it all go away and to help you feel good about yourself
again. Maybe even to feel good about yourself for the first time.
You want to wake up tomorrow morning and feel like the person
you've always wanted to be — you just aren't sure how. Sure, I
could tell you that you will wake up tomorrow as exactly the person of your dreams and nothing shy of it, but if I did, I'd be lying
to you. What I can tell you, though, is that what you want to be
and more is all possible for you — with the help of a little magic.

Now, I'm not trying to sell you a magic pill or any potions, for
that matter. What I am trying to sell you is absolutely nothing at
all — for the magic you seek is deep inside you already; you just
haven't realized it yet. Or maybe you have, but you've considered
the thought mere and utter craziness and have ignored anything
remotely close to your intuition. You've gone through life doing

pretty OK, but you want to do better. In fact, you want to do more than just OK; you want to do great. I'm here to show you that all of this is possible, and I'm here to help you achieve it. Throughout this book I'll guide you with real-life examples from real-life people, myself included, of what you can do to change your life. The chapters are structured to give you direction and action tools for each step of the way. If you're new to spirituality — or magic, as I call it — welcome! If you've been around the block but haven't been able to fully achieve your goals, welcome back! We are all lifelong learners, and there will forever be a plethora of knowledge to draw from for continuous growth. I'm here to help you take a chunk out of it in order to live a happier, healthier, more fulfilled life.

You're here because you want to feel powerful and magnetic and alive. You aspire to create a life you desire and not a life you think you should be living because someone said so. You wish to take back your power from those who seem to control your every move and thought because they said, "It's what's best for you." This book will get you clear on your aspirations in life so you can grab them and take back what's yours. It's about having the strength and courage to be happy and live a life fulfilled, one with no regrets, no anxiety attacks, no stress, and no worry. Does that sound a bit scary to you? A bit exciting? A bit of both? Well, it should. It means you yearn for it, but you just aren't sure if it's possible for you.

Maybe you've been down this road many times and you've failed, and now you're asking yourself, *Why should this time be different?* You've faced setbacks and questioned whether the success you want is really possible for you. Perhaps you've thought about pursuing your dreams but fear caught you by the throat. Maybe you've toyed with the idea but were too afraid to go through with it; but here's your chance. This time is different because you've had enough. You want a great life, but more than just wanting one, you *deserve* a great life.

This book will get you prepped up and ready to receive what is waiting for you on the other side. Do you want to learn how to do magic and live a fulfilled life? Great. You're ready to manifest your dreams into your living reality? Amazing. But you have to make a decision that you're going to do this thing and do it fully, wholeheartedly, and lovingly. It's deeper than just wanting and hoping and wishing. It's more intense than just thinking about it. Because without making a firm decision to move forward, you'll forever be stuck in the position you're in right now.

As harsh as that may sound, it isn't nearly as brutal as being in the same situation, time after time, doing the same thing over and over again, and expecting radically different results. That's just insane. The good news is, I am here to help you. I believe in the saying "You can give a man a fish and feed him for a day, but if you teach a man to fish, you feed him for a lifetime." That's my goal: to teach you, for a lifetime, how you can change your life holistically, on all levels, and live the life you've always dreamed of.

I want you to know that it's OK to be you. It's OK to wake up and be uniquely different from everybody else. To look different from everybody else. To feel different. Because you are different. You're incomparable, and you are magic. No one else in this world is you. No one else has the exact same distinct knack that you have, and that's why you're exceptional and essential in this world. It's OK to want to have a different life than what you have now, or change your career, or start a business, or do whatever it is that you want to do! There are no rules that say you must conform to a box. You were born to stand out and born to let your power shine.

I've changed my career more times than I can count. I've been a home healthcare worker, a recruiter, an IT consultant, and everything that I thought I wanted to be. I produced my own TV show, I modeled, I designed clothes, I owned a boutique, and now I'm a writer, helping people change their world to live the life of their dreams. There. Are. No. Rules. You can do whatever you put your mind to. You just have to believe in yourself and believe in the power of your special magic.

In my journey to spirituality, self-love, inner work, Source, the Universe, God, Jesus, or whatever you'd like to call it (because it's all the same), I realized I did one thing consistently: I kept an open mind. This is something that I will need you to do to make this book work for you: keep an open mind. If what you've done in the past hasn't worked for you, it's time to try something new. It's super, super important that your mind stays open to new possibilities and new perspectives. I'm going to be right here with you every step of the way. If you truly want to live a life fulfilled, you need to take a walk with faith and open your mind and heart to radical new experiences.

Whether you know it or not, the world needs you right now; the world needs what you have. The world needs your smile, your tenacity, your humor, your zest for life, your originality, your kind heart, and your awareness. The fact that you've purchased this book means that you are aware there's something in your life that needs to shift, and you've already made the first step toward radical greatness.

How to Use This Book

At the end of each chapter, you will see sections titled Magic Action, Magic Moment, and/or Go Even Deeper. These are tools meant to help you get the most out of this book and take the appropriate aligned action to get to where you want to be in this life faster. They're vital to your success in reaching your manifestation goals.

Here's a brief overview of what each section means and how you can apply it to your life.

Magic Action

Magic Actions are exercises that require you to take an aligned actionable step. Yep, that means you have to do something in order to reinforce what you're learning in this book. Yes, you need to take action to get to where you want to be (I'm talking to you, procrastinators). But don't worry, all the Magic Actions are pain-free, and none will take up your entire day, I promise.

Magic Moment

These sections offer affirmations for you to recite in order to reinforce your new ways of thinking. Statements such as *Everything will always work out for me* and *I am the source of abundance in my life* are affirmations I say daily. When you take the time every day to repeat these affirmations and others that speak to you, you help your brain form new habits that will change your life for good.

Go Even Deeper

Because I am rooting for you to manifest your dream life, I've created something special just for you. To help you reinforce what you're going to learn throughout this book, I've recorded what I call Creative Imaginings. Creative what? Yeah, I know, it does sound a bit woo-woo, but that's because it is (wink, wink). Creative Imaginings are audios that will help you change your old habits to new ones (more on this in chapter 1). These audios are specific to the chapter they come at the end of, so please listen to them in order. They will help you remove old habits and create the life you never even thought possible for yourself.

Consider this book as your guide, your toolbox, and all you'll need to make the shift from where you are right now to where you want to be.

PART 1

You Are
MAGIC

Chapter 1

Your Dreams *Can* Come True

All our dreams can come true
if we have the courage to pursue them.

— WALT DISNEY, American Filmmaker,
Master Manifester, Dream Maker

Let me ask you a serious question: Do you believe in magic? The kind that turns nightmares into dreams and thoughts into things you have wanted to see, live, and breathe in your everyday life? I remember once upon a time when my life wasn't a fairy tale. I hadn't thought of it for so many years, I had to search for it in the attic of my mind and dust it off to bring it up to you today. It's necessary for you to know about my past and how I created my present reality, so you can too. Let me tell you the story of when I used my magic to change my life.

I was an inner-conflicted person. I'd say yes to things I wanted to say no to. I'd go out of my way to please people just so they'd like me, even though I'd get nothing in return from them. I thought of myself as stuck and mired in feelings of low self-worth. I wanted to change my life, but I wasn't sure how to.

All this hit me in my early twenties, when I found myself trapped in a relentless cycle of depression, isolated in my apartment, unable to envision the life I truly desired. Contemplating a future devoid of passion, I teetered on the brink of settling for mediocrity. Broke, unhappy, and unfulfilled, I made lists of aspirations that stretched endlessly: lose weight, secure a higher-paying job, furnish my apartment, pay off my debt, and (perhaps most crucially) learn to love myself. I felt so lost, as if I were falling down an endless black hole with no way out.

One day, as I aimlessly browsed Craigslist for a distraction, the Universe sent me a sign. Amid the myriad of ads, one headline stood out: "ISO Female Workout Partner." A subtle yet undeniable ping within urged me to respond, despite the post being a month old. Hours later, an email notification lit up my screen, and soon phone numbers were exchanged. This fateful action led me to meet Greta, an encounter that would change my life.

Greta resided in Northville, Michigan, an idyllic town I had always dreamed of living in. As I pulled up to her stunning estate, I marveled at its immaculate beauty, overwhelmed by the trust she had placed in me, a stranger from Craigslist. Her welcoming embrace felt like a reunion with a long-lost sister, filling me with an inexplicable warmth. In that moment, it was as if the Universe whispered, "We've got you, Chloe. You have a purpose here, a reason to live and thrive."

With Greta, I felt a curious connection, as if we were destined to cross paths. We engaged in a deep conversation, and it soon became clear that she, too, sought transformation in her life. She longed for a sense of purpose that transcended monetary wealth.

Our meeting marked a turning point. Greta's luxurious home and warm hospitality left an indelible mark, igniting a spark within me. She epitomized the life I aspired to lead — one of wealth, small-town charm, and lush greenery. The thoughts of low self-worth that had plagued me vanished; I had a newfound reason to live, to thrive, even if I didn't yet know how.

As our friendship blossomed, Greta guided me toward

self-improvement and encouraged me to appreciate my existing blessings: a home, a car, and a job, even if the job I had didn't align with my passions. She urged me to explore new interests and career paths that would bring fulfillment and financial security. Though I didn't realize it at the time, she was becoming my mentor and guiding light.

Over the years, Greta's influence reshaped my life. She introduced me to her inner circle of successful individuals, who taught me discipline, perseverance, and the importance of pushing past my limits. Together, we embraced a rigorous fitness routine, fostering physical strength and mental resilience. I overcame procrastination, started a profitable side hustle, and confronted my inner demons, releasing pent-up anger and blame.

The overwhelming sadness that had plagued me vanished, replaced by inspiration and happiness. I stood on the precipice of becoming the Chloe I had buried deep inside. Greta's presence in my life was a transformative force, lifting me from despair and propelling me toward self-discovery and empowerment.

Rather than envy, Greta's success served as an inspiration. She demonstrated that her achievements were within reach for someone like me, and I embraced the opportunity to learn, grow, and reclaim my life. Though Greta didn't know it, her kindness and guidance pulled me out of the abyss, redirecting my focus toward gratitude, self-improvement, and the pursuit of my dreams.

The moral of the story is that I was inspired by Greta, took the necessary aligned action steps to get out of a deep, dark depression, and created opportunities for myself that weren't there before. I knew that if I wanted to get different results in my life, I needed to become the change I wanted to see.

It didn't matter what my circumstances were. It didn't matter that I didn't know *how* I was going to change. Things didn't work out just because of luck or some premonition. Things worked out because I used my *magic*. Though I had been spiraling in depression, I still took action. I still browsed the job boards and Craigslist for opportunities to help me get out of my situation. And though the post I had clicked on that day was not for a job, it turned out to be for so much more. It gave me a connection that allowed me not only to create a second stream of income but to tackle the other issues in my life (losing weight, getting fit, taking responsibility for my actions, owning my mistakes). I looked at the problem and took action steps to help me get out of my soul-crushing gloom and into the light.

So now you might be asking, *How can I use my magic to get what I want?* Your question came right on time. I'm going to show you throughout the coming chapters exactly how to do that. But first, you need to understand some guiding principles and lay a sound foundation, so everything you learn will stick like glue. Cool? Let's dive in.

How to Use Your Magic

Our minds are governed by two parts: the *subconscious mind* and the *conscious mind*.

The conscious mind is the part that is awake to the world around us and that we actively use for thinking, perceiving, and making decisions in our daily lives. This is the part of our mind that we are aware of and can control.

The subconscious mind is the part that has been gathering information since we were babies. Without our noticing it, it uses this information to bring things into our lives. Our beliefs, our unfiltered thoughts, and our entire lives are being recorded by our subconscious mind.

This part of our mind is in control of what happens in our lives. We think we are in control of our mind, but really it's our subconscious mind that runs the show.

Let me give you some examples.

If you struggle with money or wonder why there always seems to be a lack of money in your life...

- You've probably been exposed to people who have a scarcity mentality or a lack of something.
- Growing up, your family always struggled with money and never had enough.
- You feel you aren't worthy of having money or certain things in your life because someone conditioned your mind to believe this.
- You buy what you want instead of taking care of your bills.
- You've been conditioned to believe that money is evil and you should buy only what you need — anything else that you desire is "bad."
- You've been conditioned to believe that money is taboo and talking about money is rude.

If you struggle with finding the perfect partner or seem to attract only a certain type of partner, a type that doesn't ever work out for you...

- Maybe you attract cheaters or narcissists or controlling people.
- Your partner repeatedly tells you that you are worthless and you'll never find anybody better than them.
- You feel the need to change your partner or "make them better."
- You blame yourself constantly for problems in your relationship; you feel that everything is your fault.
- You feel you aren't good enough for your partner and that they will leave you for someone else.

If you struggle with losing weight, and no matter what diet you try or supplement you take, you can't seem to keep the weight off...

- Deep down inside you may not love yourself for the person you are *right now.*
- You may have been criticized your entire life about your weight, and you feel sad about it.
- You may feel that you will never lose weight and have given up hope.
- You compare yourself to others and feel less worthy than you truly are.

There are countless reasons why so many of us struggle through life with no idea as to why. Maybe you've gotten so tired of struggling that you've given up and have accepted that this is how your life is fated to be. Well, I've got news for you: it's not.

At work here are many deeply rooted issues that are ingrained within the subconscious mind. Your sorrows could be from years of torment or feeling *a lack of something* or being told that *there isn't enough money* or that *it doesn't grow on trees.* Whatever the reasoning is, your subconscious mind took this information and developed it into a *belief* — something that you consider true, though it may not be the *truth.*

If your subconscious mind believes that money is a struggle, it will make money a struggle for you in your life. The same goes for weight loss, attracting love, and any other area in your life where you're stressed.

So now you may be asking, *OK, I understand that my limiting beliefs are in my subconscious mind, but how do I get rid of them?* The short answer is: Stop believing in the lies that have been fed to your subconscious. The way to do this is by becoming aware of your thoughts and questioning your beliefs.

Here's a quick tool you can use to keep yourself in check when it comes to your thoughts:

Thoughts + Feeling = Your Reality

Let me break it down for you: simply put, *thoughts equal things.* Physical things, mental things, emotional things, and all kinds of things that turn up in your life.

Take my dear and very attractive friend Laila, for instance. Laila is in her midthirties, and for as long as I've known her, she's always been engaged. She's notorious for breaking off engagements right before the wedding day. I call her the Runaway Bride. When we first met, she was engaged to be married to a guy she'd been going out with for a few months. Then a month later, she called off the wedding because, she said, "he wanted to sleep with me before marriage, and when I wouldn't, he cheated on me." She had told him up front she wouldn't have sex with him until after they were married. She didn't believe in sex before marriage and preached about it to anyone who'd listen. As she told me about ending the engagement, she had a look of uncertainty in her eyes, as if she wasn't sure why she had gotten engaged to this untrustworthy man.

Six months later, after *another* broken engagement, a stranger called me and said he was a "good friend" of Laila's. "We're having a dinner for La's birthday, and I know you guys are tight. Come through for her surprise dinner Friday night?" He had a smooth voice, and I thought to myself, *Why haven't I heard of you before, "good friend"?* Friday night arrived, and I found myself at Andiamo's in Livonia, Michigan, with a gift bag in one hand and balloons in the other. A tall, dark, and handsome man greeted me with open arms and a kiss on each cheek. "Chloe! You're right on time — she should be here in fifteen minutes." As the stranger pulled out my chair and introduced me to everyone, I couldn't help but feel a bit odd.

"So where do you know Laila from?" I asked him.

"From the church," he said, his pearly whites glowing from ear to ear. "I went through La's phone, and I just reached out to all her recent contacts and invited them to her birthday dinner. I assumed you're tight with La because you were one of the last people she called."

Now it all made sense to me. He wasn't a "good friend," he was her *boyfriend.* But why hadn't she mentioned him to me before? Laila and I were close, and she usually talked to me about who she was dating.

Fifteen minutes passed, and in strolled Laila. She looked stunning in a white, knee-length, A-line dress with gold kitten heels and a gold clutch. Her "good friend" ran to her yelling, "Surprise!" as all of us waited to give her hugs and kisses. She sat down next to me, beaming from ear to ear. After the hype calmed down, I reached over and asked Laila who the "good friend" was. Her cheeks blushed red as she looked down at her dress and whispered, "He's just a friend that I've been seeing." She didn't seem too thrilled about him.

Unfortunately, moments later, that didn't stop her from saying, "Yes" when he suddenly got down on one knee and asked her to marry him. Her expression changed to a gleeful smile from the solemn look she had just given me shortly before.

Several months later, Laila and the "good friend," whose name I never could remember, broke it off. When I asked her what happened, she said he was seeing someone else because she wouldn't sleep with him. See the pattern? Though she was drop-dead gorgeous, she attracted men who took advantage of her. She thought that because they were "churchgoing men," they would respect her wishes to not sleep together until marriage — but deep down inside she believed that she could only attract men who would cheat on her because she wouldn't sleep with them. Laila had a scarcity mindset, a fear that had been instilled in her subconscious mind, whether it had been embedded during adolescence or more recently. In other words, she *expected* men to cheat on her, then she always broke off the engagement.

The last time I saw Laila was at my own wedding. She had just gotten out of another engagement with another "good friend" from church. She asked me how I met my husband, and when I told her it was sheer magic, she looked at me like I had lost my mind — but with a bit of curiosity in her eyes. Sadly, as many times as I've tried to help Laila overcome her mental blocks to attracting love, she has continued to revert to her old ways and hasn't yet embraced her magic.

I've known Laila for over ten years now, and in that time frame, I've overcome plenty of adversity. I've gotten myself out of an abusive relationship and healed my heart, found myself, and discovered love again. Now, you may be thinking that the reason Laila can't find love is that she wants to wait until she's married to give up the goodies. I'm here to tell you, that simply isn't true. Sex has nothing to do with finding her ideal partner. Laila doesn't believe that she's *worthy* of finding the right partner who will wait for her. If Ciara, a Grammy Award–winning singer, can convince Russell Wilson, an NFL quarterback, to abstain before marriage, then Laila and any other person can attract the same quality in a partner. What Laila lacks is an understanding of the essence of what abstaining before marriage can provide for her.

For you to attract something, whether a partner or a puppy or a brand-new car, you need not only to set the intention but also to understand and practice feeling the essence of what that thing will give you. When I say "essence," I simply mean the quality of something.

Let's take my girl Jaya, who wanted a new home. I asked her, "What would having a new home provide for you?" She said she wanted a home in the suburbs to gain a better quality of life for herself and so her kids could be influenced by the children of parents who were successful. In other words, Jaya's *intention* was to have a new home in the suburbs, and the *essence* of having that was equivalent to her having peace of mind.

Intention + Essence = Manifestation

When focusing on attraction, it is extremely important to be clear on your intention. Be crystal clear on what you're asking to receive. It's just like when you're placing an order at a restaurant. The waiter asks, "Do you want a soup or a salad?" and you say you want a soup. The waiter then says, "We have minestrone, tomato basil, and chicken noodle," and you choose minestrone. You are crystal clear on your order.

- *Intention* means you have crystal clarity on what you're asking for (a new, single-family, four-bedroom, four-bathroom home in a quiet neighborhood in the northern suburbs of Detroit)
- *Essence* is knowing what quality or qualities this home fulfills (to provide peace of mind and a better quality of life)
- *Manifestation* is your desired outcome (a new home in Rochester Hills, Michigan, nestled in a cul-de-sac across from the park)

Creating Your Manifestation List

It's time to create your manifestation list, which you'll be using for your first Magic Action. This is a list of everything you want to manifest, big and small. Your manifestation list will be as unique as you are. When creating your list, get super specific on what you want to have show up in your life. It's important that you focus on the essence of what you want your envisioned result to feel like and include all your must-haves and non-negotiables.

In fact, make two lists: one list for your big, 'bout it dreams and another for minor manifestations you want to call in. Small wins give us momentum for larger goals. Here are some examples to get you going.

Sample Big, 'Bout It Dreams List

Dream home: lake house

- $2,500 per month payment
- Single-family home
- Newly updated
- Hardwood floors
- View of the lake throughout house
- Quiet neighborhood
- Friendly neighbors
- Gated community
- Excellent school district for the kiddos

Career: brand-new job

- Analytical role
- Flexible work schedule
- Monthly salary of $12K
- Excellent healthcare benefits
- Unlimited time off
- Fully remote role
- Fun team and atmosphere
- Ability to focus on hobbies and side hustle after work

Love life: dream partner

- Sexy AF
- Trustworthy
- Taller than me
- Genuine
- Likes my friends and family
- Gets along great with kids
- Zero baggage
- Stable and secure career
- Has good credit

- Wants to be married one day
- Attentive
- Forgiving
- Loyal
- Enjoys outdoor activities and luxury travel
- Is a stand-up person

Sample Minor Manifestations List

- Winning a $1,500 gift card for Saks Fifth Avenue
- Getting an unexpected discount at a high-end store
- Finding a pair of rag & bone jeans for under $40
- Getting a free lunch
- Buying a pair of Apple AirPods Pro for under $100

Remember in the introduction when I told you you'd see exercises called Magic Action, Magic Moment, and Go Even Deeper throughout the book? These exercises are meant for you to practice; they give you ways to do the work and see the results. Here's your first Magic Action. Take the aligned steps to help you get closer to your manifestation.

MAGIC ACTION

Manifesting Your One Goal into Your Reality

From your manifestation lists, write down one goal you'd like to work toward and achieve during your time with this book. Pick one goal and one goal only. Choose something you believe you can accomplish and have faith in achieving. Keep in mind what we discussed in this lesson.

1. *Work on removing limiting beliefs that were instilled in you from childhood.* These might be beliefs around

money, scarcity, limited resources, shame, unworthiness, or anything that holds you back. Always know that
unlimited resources are available to you in this world.
Just as there is unlimited air for us to breathe, there is
unlimited abundance for every single human being on
this earth.

2. *Know that your thoughts become your world and that
you must make a conscious effort to think only in terms
of what you want.* Create your world with the thoughts
of what you want to see in your world. Thoughts such
as *I hate this job, No one will ever want me, I'm too fat*,
and *I'm not good enough* will only bring you more of the
same. Change those thought patterns by telling yourself,
*I will work in a job doing what I love, I attract the per-
fect partner into my life, I love myself*, and *I am enough*
instead.

   Along the same lines, remove the words *can't, won't,
could have, should have*, and *don't* from your vocabulary.
(For example: *I can't have money, Money won't come to
me*, etc.) Those words no longer exist in your world. Replace those words with positive mantras: *Money comes
easily and effortlessly to me, Money is in abundance in
my life*, and *I attract money effortlessly*.

3. *Think of what you're asking for as something that has
already happened.* Cool, right?! Let's go back to the
example at the restaurant. You put out your intention
(placing your order with the waiter); you focus on your
intention's essence (the items in your order and the qualities they provide to you); and you receive your manifestation (receiving your order). Think of the Universe in
that same sense.

4. *Clearly imagine what it feels like to receive what you've
asked for.* Think right now for a second about what it

feels like to eat ice cream. Imagine the salty-sweet taste of butter pecan (or your favorite flavor) on the tip of your tongue and the crunch of the waffle cone as you take a bite. Feel what it feels like to eat that ice cream. Are you happy? Can you see yourself laughing or telling yourself, "Man, this is good!"? Feel the feeling. Now imagine that you just bought your dream house. What does it feel like to be handed the keys to the house of your dreams? Are you smiling? Are you so happy that you're at a loss for words? Wait, are those tears? Feel that! This is how we bring what we want into our world: by feeling it.

5. *Just do it.* I know these steps may seem silly at first. They may even seem weird, but trust me — this is what every successful person has done and continues to do to get what they want in their lives. Things just weren't handed over to them — successful people have used their magical powers to get what they want. Now it's your turn.

Do these exercises daily, focusing on only one thing you want to bring in. In time, we'll work on manifesting bigger goals, but for now, work on a goal that you feel is easily obtainable and within your reach.

Chapter 2

Overcoming Limiting Beliefs

You don't become what you want,
you become what you believe.

— OPRAH WINFREY, American Billionaire, Changemaker, Icon

It is so unfortunate that some people live in an illusion based on somebody else's beliefs. Have you ever thought about it? If you had grown up with no outside influence over your life, what would be different about your life today? Would you be living your dream life by now? Would your view on how you should live be different?

Would you be in the Hollywood Hills or Baja California? Maybe in a house on the beach? Maybe with a private jet to fly you across the world? Or maybe in a house in the mountains? Just chilling on your back patio, watching the sunset without a care in the world? What would it be?

I remember when I was in my early twenties, living paycheck to paycheck and kicking myself because I wasn't a millionaire yet like I had promised myself I would be when I was eighteen. Instead, I was working at a low-paying job, trying to figure out where my life went wrong. I thought I was doing everything right: I'd apply to what to me were high-paying jobs that paid at least twenty-five dollars an hour in commissions for selling cable and internet door-to-door. I'd get telemarketing jobs that paid nine dollars an hour plus bonuses if I hit my quota every day. I believed that if I worked hard, I'd make a lot of money.

That's what I had been taught. These values had been instilled in me through my family, the parents of friends, random adults who would try to tell me how to live my life but who were equally broke, and what I saw on TV. All my friends' parents worked in jobs they didn't like. Whether they were chefs at a Coney Island or working in an office with a manager they couldn't stand, they always complained. From my childhood I learned I would grow up to find a job I hated and work there for as long as I could to qualify for a pension and *then*, thirty years later, I could enjoy life in retirement.

When I grew up off Dexter Avenue and Joy Road in Detroit, I didn't think about money. I knew that my family wasn't rich, but I also knew we weren't poor. We weren't begging for food or living with our lights off and no water. I knew of people who were, and I never wanted us to be in that situation. My brother and I went on trips as kids and traveled outside the country, but we didn't grow up with trust funds, knowing that our futures were financially secure.

I wasn't raised around wealth, nor did I have any wealthy white friends (or Black friends for that matter) whose parents belonged to the country club and who never had to worry about money for a single day in their lives. I grew up in a rough neighborhood, where kids who were barely ten years old were hurt or killed in drive-by shootings. I remember one friend who'd come over to my house and we'd play school on the front porch; I was always the teacher. And then one day, my brother told me he was shot and killed while riding his bike. It was so sad. Even though these stories happen every day all around the world, we don't realize how true they can be until we experience them ourselves.

There was a feeling of lack all around me. By my early twenties, I knew that I wanted to live a better life, but when you don't have the resources or the tools or even understand how to use the resources and tools you already have, how do you change your environment from one that lacks to one that thrives? I knew that money could be made. I just couldn't figure out how I could make the type of money I wanted to make to live the kind of life I wanted to live.

It was unclear to me at that age that money was energy. I just knew I needed it to pay my bills. I used to count how much money I had for gas just to make sure I could make it from point A to point B. I was broke and unhappy, and I was in my early twenties — these years were supposed to be *the best years of my life*. But if all you know is what you know and there isn't anyone to guide you to make better choices, how do you get out of survival mode and change your life into one that is prosperous?

The point I was missing was that making money was not my problem — tapping into the flow of money was my problem. All the people I spent my time with were poor. They didn't live rich lives like the rappers I saw on TV. They didn't fly on private jets or first class in commercial, nor did they drive Cadillacs or Benzes. Everyone around me was broke, and I no longer wanted to be. I knew from that point on, I would try to change my life — I just didn't know how I would go about it.

It happened for me a couple of years later, in my midtwenties, when a friend I'd met in one of my crappy low-paying jobs sat with me one day after work. We talked about our lives and how we wished they could be better. Then he shared something with me that changed my life forever. He told me to go on YouTube and look up a motivational speaker named Earl Nightingale and listen to what he had to say. He said the video was thirty-two minutes long but would be the best thirty-two minutes of my life. For those of you who don't know, Earl Nightingale was a prominent American radio personality, author, and motivational speaker in the 1950s and '60s. He talked about personal development and how we can use our minds to change the way that we live.

The video on YouTube is called "The Strangest Secret." I listened to that lecture as soon as I got home, and I have to tell you, it did change my life. "We in America," Nightingale says, "are extremely fortunate to live in the richest land that ever existed on the face of the earth. A land of abundance and opportunity for everyone." He gave an example of one hundred men who began their lives with similar economic backgrounds at the age of twenty-five. These men were excited about life and looked at it as an adventure; all of them believed they would be successful. But by the time the men were sixty-five, only five out of the one hundred would make it to financial success. "Why do so many people fail in life?" he asked. People fail, he said, because they simply don't think. In other words, people don't use the power of their minds to create the lives they want to live. The majority of folks don't tap into their magic.

Because I had been seeking knowledge I didn't have or understand, it came to me in an unexpected form — through a friend — in a way I *did* understand. Because of what my friend told me, I was able to catapult my journey not only to self-discovery but to a life of abundance and joy.

After I heard that lecture the first time, I listened to it every day, several times a day, and I learned something new each time. And from that moment on, I knew that I would dive into every book and other resource I could find to help me understand the power of my untapped potential and how I could use it to create the life I wanted to live. Then things just started happening to me. As I mentioned in chapter 1, I was able to overcome a downward spiral and create abundance in my life when I was on the brink of giving up. My life became drastically better in less than a year and continued to improve year after year. After a while I didn't even recognize myself anymore, because my way of thinking had completely changed. The way I thought about money changed, because I finally knew how it worked.

One thing we have to understand is that money is energy. It is just another form of energy or a resource that we need to survive and live in this world. Just like when you don't pay your light bill, the electricity gets shut off — because you didn't tap into the flow to continue that circulation of energy — the same is true for money. To create more money, you need to tap into the flow of it and circulate it.

Let me break it down for you further. When you create wealth, whether that's by getting a job or by starting a business that is generating money, you are tapping into an already existing pool of money. Energy is ever flowing, and money is a type of energy. When you make money at your job or business, you aren't taking it away from someone else — you're tapping into a flow of money that already exists. The Universe is an abundant source of energy; therefore, because money is energy, the Universe is an abundant source of money.

As a kid I'd overhear adult conversations about money, and it seemed as if it was a struggle to pay the bills. This made me self-conscious about spending; it was my perception that there was a lack of money, and I didn't want to play a role in it. Whenever new Jordans came out and my mom would ask me if I wanted a pair, I'd say no because I didn't want her money to go to waste on a pair of shoes for me. What I wanted wasn't as important in my eyes as what I thought she needed. I wanted her to be taken care of, and that was my way of taking care of her: by saying no to things I really didn't need. My brother, on the other hand, didn't have a problem with getting a new pair of Jordans every week! Once, my mom drove us to Canada for new Jordans for my brother because they didn't have them anywhere in the Metro Detroit area. I also recall my brother doing something to irritate me one day when we were kids at Belle Isle and me taking one of his precious Jordans and throwing it into the Detroit River.

Sibling rivalry.

My point is, if you've ever felt a lack of money or as if it will run out, it won't. It's impossible. Money is simply energy, and you just have to tap into the flow of energy to create the wealth you desire. If you're thinking about how much you hate your job and how it will never provide you with the life you want to live, change that thought pattern: think instead of how grateful you are to have a job and how it has gotten you this far in life. It has created a flow of energy that is allowing you to live how you currently live. Once you appreciate what you already have, you then become more magnetic to create what you want. You can't go through this life hating and loathing. That will only attract more of what you don't want: hateful situations, jobs you loathe, and even people you don't like.

Remember what we talked about in chapter 1?

Intention + Essence = Manifestation

The same applies to money. First, you have to focus on your intention (tapping into a flow of more money). You then feel into the essence of your intention (creating a successful business that allows you to travel to a new destination each month). Finally, you receive your manifestation (a successful online business that generates enough money for you to travel every single month to a new place in the Pacific Northwest and the Canadian Rockies).

You have a limitless power already inside you. You don't need any validation from God, Jesus, Buddha, Shiva, or whomever you worship or don't worship to tap into it. It is already there, waiting for you to use it. It is yours by birthright.

I wish I'd known this back in my teenage years — hell, back

when I was a little girl. I feel like my life would have been drastically different early on. I just didn't know the right questions to ask or whom to ask for that matter. My family didn't like talking about money around me and my brother, but my friends' parents did. I knew how much each of my friends' parents' paychecks were because my friends told me. I used to think they were rich, but in reality, they were far from it. They played the lottery every week, hoping they'd hit it big, but they never did. They relied on hope and a wish to win, but there was never any intention behind their actions.

By now, you're probably thinking, *OK, I get it about the flow of money, but how do I tap into it?* I'm glad you asked.

To tap into the ever-flowing energy of money, you first need to uncover and unblock the subconscious mind, which is holding you back from receiving an unlimited flow of money. Remember in chapter 1 when we talked about how our minds are governed by two parts, the conscious mind and the subconscious mind? The conscious mind is the part that we are aware of and that notices what is happening right now, in the present moment. Like how you are aware of yourself in this moment reading this book. It is in control of how we process information and how we experience the present. The subconscious mind is where all your beliefs, feelings, habits, and thoughts live. It influences your behavior on the basis of what has been instilled in you since childhood.

To unblock our ever-flowing source of money, we need to dig deep into the false beliefs that have been instilled in us by our subconscious minds. Your false beliefs may stem from a lack of money you felt as a kid (like I did). It may be that you grew up with limited resources and your family had to hustle to survive. Maybe you were told it was rude to discuss money and you should never tell anyone how much you have, so they won't think of you as rich or as a threat to them. Your false beliefs can be anything. Whatever the blockages are, you need to clear them out to start your flow. If you don't release these blockages, your magic simply won't work at its full potential. To tap into an ever-flowing network of abundance, connect with your untapped magic and allow it to roam free.

To create abundance, you must practice unlimited thinking. This means that you have to think in terms of how you want your life to be, as if not even the sky is the limit. What would your best life look like? What would you do every day? What kind of house would you live in, and what type of car would you drive? Would you hire a driver to take you around because you can't stand to drive? When I was in my early twenties and still trying to figure out how to tap into my magic, I would get scared to think big. I always felt I had to stay in my little box, don't make too much noise. When I'd tell someone about my dreams and ambitions, they'd laugh at me as if I'd lost my mind — as if it wasn't *possible* to have such things. They made me feel small and powerless, and then I felt as if maybe I couldn't have those things. It's even worse when your partner, whom you planned to spend your life with, is telling you that you'll fail. How do you deal with those doubts? How do you move forward when you don't know if they're right or wrong? You bench their ass, and you move on, that's how. Because you need only positive energy flowing in your life.

Negative energy from other people can influence your de-cisions. To eliminate the negative energy, you need to remove those situations from your life. If you can't cut those scenarios from your life just yet, you need to tell yourself often, *I have the power to create my reality.* If you are living in a reality that you don't like, remember that you created it. Not outside circum-stances or other people — you did. To change it, you need to take actions toward creating the life you love.

The great thing about tapping into your magic is that you

can change what you want at any time. In this world, you don't have to settle for less. You don't have to say, "Next time I'll ask for what I want." You can have what you want now.

The Universe doesn't know the difference between good or bad, right or wrong — it just brings to you what you ask for, whether you ask for it consciously or subconsciously. This is why is it so important to allow yourself to elevate your thinking about what is possible for you, even if it seems impossible to create right now. The more you play with unlimited thinking, the more you grow your imagination and create the energy to bring your dreams to you. The more you grow your imagination, the bigger you make the territories of going beyond what is possible for you. You open the doorway to your untapped magic of unlimited abundance.

Picture yourself having everything you want: the perfect body, a satisfying business or career, the perfect partner, money in your bank account, the most amazing home, and the car of your dreams. How would you feel? Would you feel like you've finally made it, living the life of your dreams? What about the people around you? How would this benefit them? What if everyone knew you were abundant and their lives were abundant, too? How would it make you feel if everyone close to you was also doing well? Imagine what it would mean to all of humanity if everyone had the opportunity to live an abundant life, without starving or worrying about shelter. How different would the world be in your eyes? I challenge you to ask for more not only for yourself but for everyone.

Let's say you've been wanting a better job. Instead of wanting a better job only for yourself, also picture that everyone else who wants a better job receives one as well. When you think in unlimited terms, you're able to create an unlimited flow. You create more abundance for yourself when you help others, whether that's by expressing gratitude, showing your love, or giving a meal to someone hungry on the street. I must warn you, though: never give with the intention of getting something back. When you give, give freely, as if no one is watching. It honestly only counts when you give because you genuinely care. Practicing this will help you understand that the Universe has true abundance, enough for everyone. There isn't a shortage of resources. There is enough to go around for everyone. As you expand your thinking to include others, you open up an even larger flow of abundance for yourself.

You can use your magic by understanding that unlimited thinking is more than just thinking *about* something — it's being able to think creatively and allowing yourself to be open to all that you want and all that you might have. It also means being open to receiving something that may be a pleasant surprise, as sometimes what you ask for may arrive in a bigger and better package than what you expected.

Let's take my friend Marquis, who was a client of mine. He decided that he no longer wanted to work a job. Instead, he wanted to work for himself, but he didn't know what he wanted to do. His brother, who had a cleaning company and was moving out of state, told Marquis that he could run it. However, the business wasn't doing well — clients were leaving left and right, and the company wasn't earning enough to replace his income from the job.

I advised Marquis to work on the business part-time and think about how it would feel to run a successful cleaning business. He informed me he wanted it to make enough money for him to quit his job and replace that income, but also enough to buy a house in the future. Marquis expressed his desire to find a girlfriend and eventually, if things went right, they'd get married and start a family. He aimed for a three-bedroom home with at least two bathrooms.

Working further with Marquis, I asked him to visualize his

ideal life. He envisioned being able to quit his job within the next month because the business would be doing so well that he no longer needed to work. Additionally, he mentioned a desire to work with clients who trusted and valued his services because he did a great job, and they always came back.

Within the month of us talking, the business had more than quadrupled in revenue. His brother had taught him how to run the equipment, and after a few training sessions, Marquis had done a cleaning gig at the retail store of one of his brother's clients. Marquis took his time and was thorough with the cleaning. That client liked the way that Marquis worked and hired him to clean his other stores — twenty of them in total. Four times a week.

With the increase in work, Marquis was able to hire help, quit his job, and build his business in a rapid-fire way.

But how, you ask?

Marquis got rid of his scarcity mindset. Working in a job he didn't like, he made a plan to leave once he secured another source of income. Even though he didn't know how things would happen, he believed that they would work out for him. His brother suddenly moved out of state and left the business to Marquis, which he didn't expect. And because he was open to abundance no matter the form it came in, the brother's business became his source of income. Even though the business wasn't doing well when his brother left it to him, Marquis had the mindset that he would do his best by serving others. He also visualized himself working with repeat clients who were happy with his service. And because of this, new opportunities opened for him.

When you are open to receiving, even in unexpected forms, abundance can flow easily and effortlessly into your life, sometimes in ways that are bigger and better than you asked for. Within less than a year, Marquis was able to buy the house he wanted. And later, he also found love.

To use your magic and manifest what you want, you must want something so badly that you will take the necessary action steps to get it. You can't just quit your job and then see what happens, hoping and wishing things work out. It's essential that you visualize the next steps and take the actions necessary to manifest the life that fulfills your aspirations. Make up your mind that something is worth having and that it is important enough for you to put a certain amount of energy and thought into making it work. Your intention to have something directs your energy, focusing it on your goals. That is your magical power.

Make sure to clear out the mentality of any scarcity that you may be experiencing. Whether you feel that more money is going out than coming in right now or you feel that somehow you've failed in life, you need to believe in your prosperous future and that everything will work out for you.

Everything in this world is temporary. When you experience a lack of income, a flow of income is on the horizon — and the Universe is offering you a lesson to learn from. Maybe it's a lesson on money management or on saving more money than you spend.

Whatever the lesson is, know that for every drought, an abundant flow is coming. If you're in a money drought right now, continue to magnetize money to you by focusing on your one goal, as we discussed in chapter 1, and ask yourself, *What is the lesson in this situation? Why am I experiencing this, and how can I use this experience to make better decisions in the future?* Leverage this time frame to start doing the things you've always wanted to do: learn a new skill, take a relaxing vacation somewhere you've been putting off, start working on that book you've always wanted to write, focus on getting a better career...the possibilities are endless. Maybe your job isn't as satisfying as it once was; consider the possibility of looking in a new direction for work. There is always a reason for a change in the flow of money, and there is always a way out of a money drought. You have countless resources at your disposal to help you grow in this phase. Whether new ideas begin to form in your mind or someone gives you an idea in simple conversation, treat these small whispers as guides to move you in the direction of your dreams.

The more appreciative you are about the things you currently have, the more rapidly abundance will flow back into your life. Maybe during this time you're developing new qualities: patience, gratitude, forgiveness, trust, and love. Always remember, you create what you focus on, so the more you focus on what you want and how it would feel to have it, the more quickly you will draw it to you. As you reach higher and higher levels of manifestation, you'll be able to attract what you need when you need it, and you'll be less affected by the natural cycles of money droughts.

MAGIC ACTION

Releasing Early Childhood Blockages

1. Find a comfortable place where you can be alone for ten or fifteen minutes. Sit at ease on a chair or the floor. Your spine should be upright so that energy can flow through you freely. Get quiet, close your eyes, relax, and take a deep breath in, then out. Do this three times.

2. As you keep breathing deeply and sinking into a relaxed state, think about a time as a child when you felt a lack in your life. Maybe you wanted a bicycle, but you were told that it was too expensive. You might have wished for a pair of jeans, but your family didn't have enough money to buy them for you. How did this make you feel? Dig deep to recall a time when you were told no about something you wanted because of a lack of money. Revisit this memory and the feelings you had. Please remember that

you are in a safe space, and you won't need to relive this experience if it was triggering to you. Instead, go back in time as an observer of the situation, allowing yourself a sense of detachment and security.

3. Once you recall the incident, imagine you are at a chalkboard with an eraser and wipe the memory from your mind. As you wipe it clean, let it go from you. Forgive those who told you that you couldn't have something because of a lack of money. Forgive them even if they did wrong to you, because as you forgive, you release tension and negative energy, allowing abundance to flow through you. Your parents did the best they could with the resources they had, and they are not to be blamed. Forgive them and thank them for raising you. Unleash any anger, guilt, or shame you have toward them and/or the situation and wipe it cleanly from your mind. Let go of all negative thoughts and feelings from those situations, as they no longer serve you.

4. Take a deep breath and relax your mind. You've just surrendered a major blockage from your life that has been holding you back from an ever-flowing source of energy. How do you feel? Do you feel lighter? Happier? At peace?

5. Repeat this exercise as many times as necessary to release blockages from your body. If you couldn't focus on any single situation or you felt yourself drifting, practice again until you're able to focus fully and complete the exercise. You should feel a sense of relief when you're done, as if weight has fallen from your shoulders.

You are now in a position where you can create your reality by using your magic. You can create abundance in your life without fear of there never being enough. There will always be enough.

GO EVEN DEEPER

I know it might be difficult to be happy about what you currently have, especially if you're in a position where you don't want to be. Wherever you are in life, I've created this Creative Imagining not only to help you to appreciate what you already have, but to help you achieve even greater success and catapult yourself into the life you want to be living. Please go to my website to access your Creative Imagining audio: ChloePanta.co/um-1.

Chapter 3

Mind over Matter

*The world is yours and everything in it. / It's out there —
get on your grind and get it.*

— JEEZY, American Rapper, Thug Motivator, Magic Maker

Growing up, my favorite rapper was Lil Wayne. I memorized all the lyrics to every song he ever made, and I even went to my first Cash Money Millionaires concert because he was so inspirational to me, a thirteen-year-old girl, at the time. This was back in 1999.

I'd watch him on TV, mesmerized by the flashy cars, jewels, and lifestyle in general. For a while in high school, I wanted to be a rapper, and my friends and I would come up with rap songs and practice at lunchtime. I wanted to be rich and live my life doing what I wanted, when I wanted, with millions of dollars at my disposal — just like Lil Wayne.

At the tender age of thirteen, I didn't think it would be difficult to become a rapper. All you had to do was write some songs, sound decent on a recording, and then send your mixtape off to some record studios or a producer and — voilà! — you became a rapper!

Since my plan didn't work out so well, I was always curious about how celebrities got so famous and so wealthy. It never occurred to me that they used their magic to create their reality. I just figured that these people were the chosen ones and had life easy.

After I discovered more about how to harness the power of my magic, I realized that they used their magic, too. They set an intention, focused on visualizing the essence of what they wanted, and took action to attract their manifestation. There isn't much more to it than that.

Though everyone's story is different, everyone who is famous — whether they are a rapper, an actor, a basketball player, or an influencer — had a goal, focused on that goal, and brought it to life.

Now, you might be thinking that it will take a tremendous effort to get to the level where a celebrity is, and I'll tell you: it depends. You see, we each believe that some things are true, and we each believe in certain principles. Each of us has a different experience. I know a lot of people who believe that it takes hard work to become successful. They live by the mantra "Work hard, play hard." So for them, the road to success has been difficult. If they don't work hard, they don't reap the benefits — this is what they believe in. Whether it was instilled in them from a young age or they were influenced by others, this belief became true for them.

I also know some people who believe that getting what they want is enjoyable. So everything they do is enjoyable. Whether that is creating a business, finding a life partner, or buying a house, they live their life with ease, peace, and happiness. Everything happens effortlessly for them.

How has life been for you so far? Do you find your life hard? Do you work hard and feel stressed all the time? Or is your life full of joy, calm, and serenity? If you believe in certain principles, they become true for you — whether someone else believes them or not. Just because *you* believe them, these principles become *your* reality.

One thing to note is that in this world, we all live in our own reality. Some people believe in roughing it through the storm and persevering, while others believe in running from their responsibilities when the shit hits the fan. Some people believe that they can only ever have a side hustle and never run a business full-time for themselves. Other people believe they can just go out in the world and start a business and become profitable from day one.

Have you ever done something that happened easily for you? Maybe you went through an easy job interview process and you got hired with little effort. Maybe you wanted to buy a new car and you got an amazing deal, better than the original asking price. Have you ever noticed these synchronicities? These things happened because you believed they were possible for you.

One time my husband and I were trying to sell our car. It was a lease, and we wanted to turn it in early. A week before, my husband had accidentally hit the front of the car on the corner of our garage (he had too much ice cream that day). He thought that because of the accident, the value of the car would go down and we wouldn't get the amount of money we wanted. Well, the body shop gave us a discount (which was nice because they said they usually don't), and after we got the car repaired, the insurance company didn't increase our monthly premium. When we went to a dealer in Santa Barbara to see if they would buy our car, they gave us four thousand dollars in our pocket after our lease payment. So we made a nice profit when we sold our car. None of this happened by chance. It happened because we believed it would and we felt confident that we would get what we thought the car was worth. We believed it would be an easy process, and it was. Your path to success can be easy and peaceful and joyful, or it can be treacherous and difficult and painful. The choice is up to you.

Celebrities are famous for two reasons: they take on projects that gain them the experience they need to make a name for themselves, and they believe in their power to create opportunities. That is, they have faith that a certain type of life is possible for them, and they take the necessary action steps to get there and stay there. Some celebrities from twenty-plus years ago are still in the limelight today because of their ability to adapt to changing industries and their persistence in maintaining their success by continuing to achieve milestones and win awards. They have a fundamental belief in their own worth.

Now, maybe you're wondering about people who seem to have overnight success. Maybe some influencers appear to have gained popularity out of nowhere. Those people have persuasive power that has reached the masses. Maybe they're a food blogger and their recipes have helped thousands upon thousands of people cook healthy dinners every night. Maybe they are a healer and they empower their clients to take an active role in their self-healing. Or they're a money guru who teaches folks about financial success and how to manage their money better. Whatever service they are offering, they are genuinely helping others to help themselves. And because they believe in the power of their worth and they are doing what they love, the money flows abundantly for them.

If you focus your intention on your passion, you create an overflow of money, which is energy.

Intention + Passion = Overflow of Energy

When you are connected to the Universe, Source, God, or whatever you'd like to call it (I like to use "the Universe" or "Source" or "God" interchangeably), you are connected to an overflow of energy. When you are following your soul's path to doing what lights you up and what brings you joy, you are on the path to abundance. When you are in flow, your magic becomes more magnetic.

We all operate at different frequency levels. You become much more powerful when you are in tune with the vibrational frequency that matches that of what you desire. As the American rapper Meek Mill once sang, "It's levels to this shit." It simply means that if you don't have what you desire yet, you need to match the vibrational frequency level of what it is you desire, whether that's becoming an influencer yourself or running a successful online business or finding success as a world-renowned singer.

Vibrational frequency attracts
like vibrational frequency.

We are attracting energy around us all the time, whether we like it or not. When you're upset with someone because they've wronged you, you're attracting more of that energy to you. If you're finding yourself in the same crappy situations over and over again, it's called insanity, but it's also called your vibrational frequency level. If you want to attract experiences at a higher vibrational frequency level, you need to raise *your* vibrational frequency level.

High vibes all around.

Have you ever dated someone who seemed just as bad as the last person you dated? Maybe they were a cheater, or they took their sweet time when replying to your texts, or they didn't want to commit to a relationship because they just got out of a bad one, or they just weren't what you were looking for. Maybe they were even abusive toward you. Does it seem that you attract the same type of partner all the time? If you do, it is because you are operating at a frequency level that matches theirs. It also can mean that you feel this is the type of person you deserve to have in your life and that you can't do any better. Maybe deep down inside you feel you aren't worthy of having the partner you desire.

When you operate at a low vibrational frequency level (feeling jealous, envious, sad, worried, victimized, unattractive, unworthy, etc.), you attract other low vibrational frequency people and situations into your life. This causes conflict and unhappiness. When you operate at a low vibe level and you expect amazing things to happen to you that operate at high vibe levels (the perfect partner, more money, amazing opportunities, happiness, love for others, kindness, serenity, gratitude, worthiness, etc.), you may end up feeling disappointed. And if this has happened or is currently happening to you, there is a way to fix it.

To get what you want, you must match
the vibrational frequency of what you want.

Your vibrational frequency match is what the Universe will return to you. Maybe you've noticed that when your vibe is high, you get unexpected opportunities, you meet incredible people who are kind and caring, and everything seems perfect. This is because when you're vibing high, the Universe returns high vibes to you. When you're vibing low — well, the Universe will return that as well.

Remember, the Universe doesn't know what good or bad is or what right or wrong is. It just brings back to you what you put out. That's why you can't say, "Gimme a milli, dawg" and expect a million dollars. You need to match the vibrational frequency of that one million dollars to receive it. Get it? Got it? Good.

If you learn to vibrate at a higher frequency level and stay at that level, knowing that what you desire is coming to you even when you can't see it yet, that is when you really and truly harness the power of your magic.

So, you might be asking, *how do I raise my vibrational frequency to get what I want?* Not to worry, I'll explain that process in a minute. I get it: You want to change your life already. You're ready to quit your job and do something meaningful. You're ready to be free of the soul-sucking relationship that you're in and attract the partner of your dreams. You're ready to find your person. You want to promote gender equality and close the pay gap. You want to overcome a fear or personal challenge. You want to find inner peace, happiness, and fulfillment. You want your four acres and a mule. I know you do. I want you to have it, too. Because you deserve it, and don't let anyone tell you anything different.

But before you attract what you want, one principle that you must understand is this:

You must believe that what you are asking for is
something you can have.

If you really want a million dollars, do you believe you can have it? Or is it a pipe dream? Smoke and mirrors? If deep down in your gut you don't feel that this is something you can have today, you won't attract it to you. You first have to learn how you'll manage that kind of money, understand how you'll spend it, and imagine how it will feel to have it in your bank account. How will you use it to help others? Once you get comfortable with the thought of having a million dollars, try asking for it again. You can do this by staying connected to the Universe. Let's dive deeper into that.

How to Stay Connected to the Universe

When you're engaged with your magic, you have to be in alignment both with the energy and with the appropriate action steps to achieve what you want. You can't just think about what you want without taking any action, imagining that something will magically appear out of thin air — thoughts and actions must collaborate. It's vital that you make sure that what you want, you want wholly and fully, and that you're putting in the work to get it.

The other trick that's imperative you understand, as I mentioned above, is that you must believe that what you want will happen for you, regardless of your current circumstances. If Tyler Perry can go from living in his car to being one of the wealthiest men in showbiz, you can change your circumstances too.

When you've got the belief and the action down pat, your next step is simply to wait. Be patient and know that the thing you've asked for is coming for you. You don't need to ask for this thing over and over again. Remember, you're not pleading here. There's no judge or jury to prove your innocence to. You're simply co-creating with the Universe. Once you've done the work and every day you're naturally experiencing what it feels like to have what you want, the Universe is in motion to bring you what your heart desires.

You must keep your vibration high,
no matter what your situation is right now.

Some of you may be in a situation that seems impossible to get out of. Maybe you wake up with a feeling of doom looming over your shoulders. You feel heavy with stress and other problems in your life. Regardless of what is happening now, know that there is a way out. When you keep your vibes high, you are connecting with the Universe. When your vibes are high, you're taking actions toward your goal, and you're connected to the Universe, you become an unstoppable force.

Even when it feels hard, even when you don't want to, you *must* keep your spirits up and think only in terms of how great your life will be. It's OK to let the feelings and emotions of depression, anxiety, and sadness overcome you — but let them pass through you. Do not sulk in these feelings. Instead of sinking deeper into those feelings of dread and doom, focus on how amazing it is to be alive right now. Think about how grateful you are for all that you have now. Know that what you want is coming — you just haven't reached that point in time yet where it's physically yours. You have to continue to raise your vibration in order to raise yourself out of the situation you're currently in. The longer you sulk, the longer you'll be stuck. The quicker you shake it off and raise your head up high, the quicker you will move toward what you want. That's how it works.

How to Raise Your Vibrational Frequency

When you're trying to change your life for the better, sometimes you have to conquer your fear and trust the unknown. You must believe in the greater good — the greater good of humanity, of this planet — and that the Universe is on your side, not against you. You must leave the victim mentality in the trash. There's no room for it where you're going. Choosing faith over fear equals a fruitful life.

Choosing faith over fear = a fruitful life

You raise your vibrational frequency by first stating to yourself, whether aloud or in your mind, *I know what I desire is possible for me to have.* Not only do you say that to yourself, you 100 percent believe in it. You feel it. You imagine what it's like to have the thing you want or to be the person you want to be. Then you take the necessary action steps to get there. You must combine all three.

Affirmation + Belief + Action = Higher Vibrational
Frequency

Once you've incorporated these principles into your life, you will start to see changes happening. No matter how small they may seem at first, synchronicities will happen because you are making the necessary changes, using your magic to enhance your life. Remember, you are the co-creator of your life. The Universe is your co-pilot. You are the one flying your plane, leading your life down the path you want to go. The Universe is there to guide you and give you what you want because you're asking for it.

MAGIC ACTION

Releasing Fears

1. Get quiet for a moment and write down all the things you are fearful of.
2. Next to each item on your list of things you're fearful of, write down all the reasons why you're afraid.
3. Ask yourself the following questions about each of your fears:

   - *What is the source of the fear?*
   - *When did the fear first manifest?*
   - *Has the fear happened before? If so, what did I do to overcome it?*
   - *How does this fear affect my quality of life, emotions, and actions?*
   - *What is the worst that can happen if this fear manifests?*
   - *Why am I letting this fear stop me from moving forward with taking action?*

4. Now, for every fear you've written down, write next to it its opposite possibility. For example, if you wrote, "I am afraid of being broke," write out next to it, "I live in an abundant world full of endless opportunities. I can work on building a new stream of income from a job or a side hustle and grow from there. I know that the Universe is always supportive of me and looking out for me."

5. Take a good look at all the opposite possibilities you wrote down. Read them to yourself and believe in them fully. Feel the feeling you would have if you were living and experiencing them, and write that down too. If you wrote, for instance, "I'm afraid of losing my job and not having money," write down, "I am grateful for the job I have. I am open to change and my ability to find new opportunities. I will focus on taking aligned action to create the life I want, where this fear of insecurity will no longer have any power over me. I am living an abundant life. What I want is coming for me, waiting for me. I just have to believe in my power to attract it to me. My job is a stepping stone to greater possibilities, and I will do my best because something amazing is already in place to happen to me." Be creative with what you write. Make sure it sounds believable to you.

6. Take your pen and cross out all the negative fears one by one. As you cross out each one, consciously release that fear. Know that these fears no longer hold power over you because you can overcome them by facing them (writing them down) and then releasing them (crossing them out on the paper and wiping them out of your life).

7. Do this exercise anytime something fearful comes your way. Acknowledge its presence and then release it by creating an affirmation with its opposite possibility. By sending love to your fears, you are letting go of their hold on you. Fear is simply a place within you waiting for love.

Chapter 4

The Magic of Magnetization

*The most common way people give up their power is
by thinking they don't have any.*

— ALICE WALKER, American Novelist, Civil Rights Activist,
Pulitzer Prize Winner

Y ou have the power to change your world. It lies deep down
inside you. When you know how to properly use your magic
to create the world you want to see, you become a limitless being.

Tapping into your magic and drawing to you what you want
in life is easier than you might think. It's especially a lot easier when you use the power of your wand. Now you might be
thinking, *Wand? What is this, Harry Potter?* No, absolutely not.
What I mean by "using the power of your wand" is activating the
power of your mind. Think of yourself as magic, because you are.
Think of something you desire, that one thing we talked about
in chapter 1. Then, I want you to get quiet and concentrate on
bringing that thing you want into focus in your mind. Use your
mind to create a vision that you want to see happen in your physical world. When you activate the power of your mind — that is,
your wand — to magnetize what you want, you can draw it to you
more quickly than if you weren't using it.

A wand is simply a tool that you focus energy into. Whatever you focus on, you draw to yourself, just as we talked about in chapter 3. You work with your wand (your mind) all the time, though usually not consciously. With your thoughts, you send signals out every single day. This magic may be repelling things away from you or attracting things to you. This chapter will teach you how to use your wand consciously and create more of what you want in this life. When you use your magic properly and focus your wand with crystal clarity to bring to you what you want, you draw your desires closer.

When I use my mind as a wand, I like to think of the process as something like making a movie, where I'm the main character and the director and the wardrobe stylist all wrapped into one (because it's my life, right?). I imagine whatever it is I want, and I believe with my whole heart that that thing is real and that it's going to happen for me. I picture it first with my mind's eye in order to bring it to life in this 3D world.

I am increasingly magical, and I attract money, happiness, and serenity into my life every single day.

Let's go over some basic principles to becoming more magnetic.

Basic Principles of Magnetizing

When you are creating something new, you are manifesting something from your mind into this physical world. The basic principles of magnetizing in this section will help you get crystal clear on what you want to manifest, how to bring it into your world, and how to continue to manifest your dream life.

You are a unique being. There is no one else quite like you, and there never will be anyone who can do what you do in the exact way that you do it. This is your authentic power that you were born with. No one can take that away from you. You're special, and you're an original. Because of this, you align with certain characteristics that are true to who you really are.

Our essence is already whole.

We are already whole beings, born into this world with innate worthiness. However, our life journey often exposes us to pain, shame, trauma, and limiting beliefs imposed by external influences like family, friends, peers, colleagues, and media. As we adapt to our environment, these influences disconnect us from our true authentic selves. Because we're afraid of what people would think of us if we were to be who we really are, we've put on masks and hidden our true identity. We have not been living our lives the way they were meant to be lived. The Universe's ultimate intention is to guide us back to our authentic, whole, and worthy selves. Our responsibility is to gradually shed the layers of pain, shame, unworthiness, and trauma so that we can manifest our limitless lives.

Self-Belief = Law of Attraction

What you believe yourself to be worthy of shows up in your life. In other words, your subconscious self-beliefs in certain areas of your life (such as love, finances, career, business, etc.) shape what you attract into your life. That's why some of us feel like we can't make a certain amount of money, attract a certain partner, or change another area of our lives. It is because subconsciously we don't believe that we can.

Aligning with our innate worthiness leads to the manifestation of our desires. But whatever you are asking for, have a detachment about it. Believe me, this is so super important. You don't need to beg and plead for this thing to come to you. Know that what you've asked for is on its way and surrender to it. It's so true when they say that if you love something, let it go, and if it's meant to be yours, it will come back to you. No need to thirst over what you're asking for.

I'll give you an example. The husband and I were house hunting in sunny California. At first, we thought we'd replace our rent with a mortgage and build equity in a new home. As we saw house after house, our needs changed. Instead of a simple two-bedroom home, we decided we both needed home offices so we could work from home. We also realized that for a much larger home, we'd need to spend more money than just replacing our rent payment.

House hunting during the pandemic felt like a bit of a panic. Everybody wanted to buy a home, and we encountered flocks of people competing in bidding wars to get the home of their dreams. With each beautiful home that we saw, we were outbid. After a few weeks of searching, I found a listing that I kept going back and forth about. The house was beautiful and had everything I wanted in a home, but I just felt tired of the hustle and bustle, and I told myself if the listing was still up a few days later, I'd go check it out. However, I had a gut feeling that told me to *go check it out now*, so our real estate agent, Mark, and I went to see the home in person later that day. My husband didn't come because he had a meeting he couldn't get out of.

When we arrived, it looked like a castle, something straight out of a fairy tale book, and I fell in love with it immediately. I toured the home with Mark, and then I FaceTimed my husband and said, "This is it. This is the one." We put in an offer, and I just said, "You know what, if this is really the one, it will come." I had a detachment about this home. I didn't feel the need to "win," like I did with the other homes. A few days later, Mark told us the seller accepted our offer immediately — even though it was only a few thousand dollars over the asking price, which was *pennies* compared to the hundreds of thousands over asking that people were dishing out to be top bidders for other homes. Turns out the seller's agent's inbox had ten other offers, but ours happened to come in at the top of the queue. Now, who knows if the other offers were higher than ours? It simply didn't matter. Because when something is meant to be yours and you surrender to the possibility, it will always come to you.

Your Wand = Your Mind + Energy

When I say "magnetize," what I mean is that you are attracting to you what you want or, sometimes, even what you don't want. Think of how a penny or a bobby pin attracts itself to a magnet. Magnetizing what you want is the same principle, because when you use energy, you are generating a magnetic field. We are made up of energy, and the world we live in is powered by energy. When you use your wand to draw to you what you desire, you are using your energy by generating a magnetic field. Understand?

Magnetism = Energy + Visualization

Every time you do any of the exercises in this book, you'll notice a shift in your thoughts, ideas, and feelings. When you are manifesting something, you're working with an ever-evolving state of energy — it's always changing. You may have new ideas, and your goals may change over time; that's called life. Let's say you want a brand-new two-door coupe today, but then as you go through life, you get married, you're ready to start a family, and you realize you now need an SUV. And that's OK. Being creative, thinking of images that pop up in your mind, and having a genuinely wild imagination are typically the only tools you'll need when you're creating with energy. Everything is always evolving, and using your imagination to expand upon what feels right for you is the best way to attract what you want.

The feeling of magnetism is more important than anything else. It could be a feeling in your core, the center of your being, that tells you, *This is it.* When you feel that feeling, live in that moment, because that is your magic at work, drawing to you what you've asked for.

I am a money magnet.

The easiest way to use your wand and test out your magic is to manifest something similar to what you already have. This will get you a few wins under your belt and let you see what it feels like to succeed in creating something new. Using the minor manifestations list you created in chapter 1 is a good place to start. Doing this will give you feedback and will allow you to develop your manifesting skills. As you practice by manifesting smaller goals and get the hang of it, you can move on to larger goals.

A client of mine, Luna, wanted to manifest a new career in a different field. Thousands with jobs similar to Luna's were being laid off, and she knew it would only be a matter of time before she'd be let go, too. She told me she wanted to be ahead of the curve and asked for help with manifesting a new career, one where she'd have career stability. For as long as she could remember, she had always wanted to work in IT, but she felt intimidated and discouraged because there weren't a lot of women who worked in IT at her company — especially women of color. She also didn't have a college degree. After I helped her do some deep work on self-worth and on removing limiting beliefs, she found that the core reason she wasn't working in IT was because she was fearful of not being good enough.

Within a few weeks, her company laid her off and provided her with a nice severance package. During that time, she heard through a friend of a friend about an IT study program for underrepresented women who didn't have college degrees; it would provide them with full-time jobs upon completion. With her severance, Luna was able to sustain herself until she finished the program and then landed herself a high-paying career as a project manager.

Though Luna was fearful and wasn't sure how she'd land a new job in a career that she had no experience in, her visualization and manifestation powers outweighed her fears as she pursued her dream. She used her magic to remove the perception of fear from her subconscious mind, and she was able to practice feeling the feeling of being in her new role as well as taking the necessary action steps to obtain her new career. She up-leveled her life by stepping into her worth.

When you magnetize something, you'll begin to feel as if what you want is coming to you. It can be a gut instinct, a warm sensation in your core, or just an inner knowing. When you feel this, it is the sign that your magnetization is complete, and no more magic is needed to fulfill this goal. If you don't experience this type of feeling, it means that you still have work to do, and you need to continue to use your magic to magnetize your goal.

Developing an inner knowing comes with time — this isn't something that typically happens the very first day you start practicing manifestation. Start by practicing with small goals, such as learning a new skill or being kind to others or going to the gym on a regular basis. Whatever the goal is, practice until that goal becomes a part of your living reality. Understood? Remember:

Magnetism = Your Authentic Self

Only you will know when you've used the right amount of magic to create the results you want to see. You will have to learn to sense how much energy is needed to bring your visualizations to life. Now you might be asking, *But what if I use too much energy?* If you feel like you're straining to bring what you want into your life, what you're calling in is on a different vibrational frequency level than what you are currently operating on, and you need to continue to unblock in areas where you feel lack. The process of manifestation is effortless. It should come naturally and feel easy to you. If you are struggling to bring what you want to life, you're going against the flow of your higher path, and you still have inner work to do.

I create what I want with my magic.
Good things come easily and effortlessly to me.

Maybe you're thinking to yourself, *All right, Clo, I know how to magnetize what I want, but what if I'm not using enough energy? What do I do then?* I got you. If you feel like maybe you're not using enough energy to attract what you want or the thing that you want seems far away, it may be because, deep down inside you, that thing you want feels more like a hope and a wish than a confirmed affirmation. It may not seem real to you just yet. It also means that you are miles away from matching the vibrational frequency level of the thing it is that you want.

Before you attract something much larger than the energy you are putting out, you have to learn to match your energy to what it is you desire, just as we talked about in chapter 3. You can only attract according to your current vibrational level. If you're trying to attract one million dollars but have ten-dollar vibes, a million won't come to you. You have to match your vibe to the thing that you want. Remember, you will need to *feel the feeling of having it.* How will it feel to have one million dollars? How will it help you? How will you use it? You need to visualize yourself having a large sum and consistently think about how it would feel to have it so that you feel more and more comfortable with it. The more you do this, the deeper you tap into your power and enhance your magnetism, and the closer you get to your goal.

In addition to matching your vibrational frequency level with the frequency of what you want, you'll also need to resolve any concerns you may have about receiving it. Do you have family members who will ask you for money? If so, how will you handle those situations? What about your taxes and hiring an accountant? Have a well-thought-out plan for your million dollars before you receive it. Otherwise, you might not manage your money properly and end up back where you started.

Sometimes it takes knowing the right people to draw to you what you want. Whether that's friends who will lead you to a new job (like in Luna's case) or people who will have the connections you need to catapult you to the next level, attracting key people in your life is vital. At the end of this chapter, I want to share with you how you can use your magic to attract amazing people who will help you obtain your goals. But first, let me introduce you to someone even more important.

Your Authentic Self

Now you may be asking, *What is your Authentic Self, and how do you find it?* Your Authentic Self is already inside you. It is your guide that provides you with all the answers to the questions you may have about your life, your journey, and anything else for that matter. It is the part of you that is free of any ego; some would say it is your soul or spirit. It is the you that dances in the mirror when no one is watching or sings in the shower when no one is listening. It is who you are at your core. I call it interchangeably God, Infinite Intelligence, my Higher Self, and my Authentic Self. You can address it however you feel comfortable, with whatever words resonate for you. With your Authentic Self, there is no need to put on a mask or be anyone other than you. Your Higher Self knows your every secret and loves you for exactly who you are, where you are. It is in fact the *real you*, in your most unaltered state. Pure perfection. Here's a guided meditation to help you connect with your own deep essence.

Connecting with Your Authentic Self

To connect with your Authentic Self, you must keep an open mind and go within. In other words, get in a quiet place, close your eyes, and relax.

Imagine that you are in a beautiful place. This can be a garden, a luxury mansion, the middle of the hood — it can be anywhere you'd like, as long as it feels real and beautiful to you. Imagine that this place has stairs, and as you climb the stairs, you reach a room. Imagine what this room looks like in great detail. Is it grand? Does it have marble countertops? Is that an oak hardwood floor you're standing on?

Now, imagine that sitting in the middle of the room is you in your most desired state, in all perfection — your Authentic Self. Imagine your regular self sitting directly across from your Authentic Self; you feel a calm easiness flowing through you. What does your Higher Self look like? What clothes is your Higher Self wearing? Nothing at all? Oh-kay, you do you. But seriously, imagine asking your Authentic Self any question you'd like to know an answer to and wait for your Authentic Self to respond. The answer might be immediate, or it may take days or longer, but a still, small voice within you will tell you the true answer to what you seek. You don't need outside validation for anything. You already know all the answers, because they lie within.

Imagine what your life would be like if you knew you had a direct connection to Source. Imagine that your Authentic Self *is* Source. In other words, you're the plug. You're the connection to everything and the gateway to your greatness. Your happiness, your wealth, your health, your inner peace. What does that feel like, knowing you have a direct connection to the most magical Source of power that has ever been created? That Source lies within you, and you can activate its power whenever you want.

Learning to connect with your Authentic Self, like building any muscle, takes time and practice. Beyoncé wasn't built in a day; don't expect your Authentic Self to give you all the answers you're looking for without practice. Take time every day to get quiet and be still. Quiet your mind and your emotions. As you master this meditation over time, you will connect with your Authentic Self easily and effortlessly, receiving the answers you're looking for. Should you apply for that new job? Should you stay in your relationship? What steps should you take to find divine freedom? The most amazing thing about connecting with your Authentic Self is that you can ask any question you want, and you will receive an answer.

I have to forewarn you, though, that the answers you receive may not always be the answers you expect to hear. Your answers may come in different forms: a song on the radio, a tiny whisper inside, a friend calling you out of the blue, a book that you happen to read. As you deepen your practice, these subtle signs will become easier to notice and decipher. Be kind to yourself as you learn to connect with your Higher Self. This journey may be brand new for you, and like all things, it takes time to master.

Now, let me teach you a Magic Action that will help you magnetize to you the people who will help you manifest your goals.

MAGIC ACTION

Manifesting Your Dream Team

1. Sit in a space where you feel comfortable. This can be your bedroom, sitting upright on your bed, or in your living room on the floor or in a chair, sitting up straight. Now, get quiet. Take a deep breath, inhaling through your nose and exhaling through your mouth. With each breath in and out, feel more and more relaxed. Repeat this breathing and relaxation pattern five times.

2. Now, close your eyes and think about your goal. What's the next step in achieving it? Think about the right people you need to connect with to help you get there. This may be a specialist to help you build your new coaching business. This could be a friend of a friend who knows the person you need to know to help you close a deal on a new house. This could be a banker to help you get the loan you need to buy the building to open your new restaurant. This is anyone who will be beneficial to you in achieving the next step toward your goal.

3. With your eyes still closed, imagine yourself connecting with this person, and they are eager to help you. Imagine having in-person meetings or going to events or meeting virtually. Imagine everything working out for you. In this step, don't focus on the *how* — leave that up to a source and power that is greater than yourself — just focus on the *feeling* of having all this happen to you. Sink deeper into that feeling and continue with your visualization of your dream coming true, with the help of this person.

4. Imagine your energy, your magic, getting stronger as you send love out to this person. As you sense this connection growing deeper, imagine this person walking into

your life, as if they were coming to you from a dream, eager and willing to help you. Thank this person for helping you to reach your goal.

5. Now imagine how it will feel after you've achieved your goal and you reach even more people. If you're a life coach, for example, imagine having an abundance of clients who are eager to work with you. Visualize a grid, and on that grid, visualize tiny hearts that light up. Imagine those hearts as your future clients, just waiting to work with you. Imagine a plethora of hearts lighting up all over this imaginary grid. How does it feel? Stay in that feeling.

6. Go deeper within and ask your Higher Self to bring these people to you. Imagine them coming into your life and helping you along your path. Imagine them feeling ecstatic from the results you provide them. Thank all these people and slowly come back to the present, opening your eyes.

✦ **GO EVEN DEEPER** ✦

Embodying your dream self, the person you've always wanted to be, can feel exciting, but it can be hard to know how to get there. Knowing yourself and fully developing into your Authentic Self can take some time, but once you've got it, you become it. To help you peel back the layers of shame, pain, unworthiness, and guilt and step into your power, I've created this Creative Imagining. Are you ready? It's time to become the person you've always wanted to be. Please go to my website to access your Creative Imagining audio: ChloePanta.co/um-2.

PART 2

Embrace Your
MAGIC

Chapter 5

Living in a State of Magic

Every great dream begins with a dreamer. Always remember, you have within you the strength, the patience, and the passion to reach for the stars to change the world.

— HARRIET TUBMAN, Freedom Fighter, Risk-Taker, Antislavery Warrior

Back in 2016, I was having lunch with my beautiful Barbadian co-worker, talking about our future selves. Richelle is a doctor who does real estate investing on the side, the type of woman who knows what she wants and goes after it.

She said to me, "Chloe, I'm going to be a wife this time next year." She pushed her glasses off the bridge of her nose and brushed her long, thick hair off her shoulders.

I looked at her like she was crazy. "What?" I said. "Girl, you're single."

"I know, I know, but I also know that I'm going to be married in a year." She was gushing and giddy, as if she was already head over heels in love with someone — like I actually was.

"OK, girl, have fun!" I took another forkful of my salad.

"You too," she said. "You gotta say it too. Come on!"

I loved my boyfriend dearly, but I never thought about the future with him. Our love was a live-in-the-moment type of thing. I never wanted to rush it. I just savored every second of it. But she got me thinking. *Hmm, maybe I should...*

So I said, "OK. I'm going to be married in the summer of next year, and it's going to be a magical wedding, small, with close friends and family."

Needless to say, my friend Richelle did indeed get married a year later. To a man who was also from Barbados and who also happened to love real estate investing as much as she did. Her wedding took place in Barbados within a year of our conversation over lunch.

And you know what?

So did mine.

On the exact date, I married the love of my life, and it's been bliss ever since.

But how? How do two young co-workers, casually talking about marriage, end up being married on the exact dates that they said they would?

Magic.

Let's dive a little deeper.

In chapter 1, we discussed how the subconscious mind operates. It's working on autopilot all the time, and even though we are not always aware of it, the subconscious influences our thoughts, actions, and feelings. It brings our inner beliefs and patterns into our outer world. In chapter 3, we looked at how raising our vibrational frequency to match that of what we desire brings us what we want in life. We also noted that choosing faith over fear equals a fruitful life:

Choosing faith over fear = a fruitful life

The two things that Richelle and I had in common at that time were that (a) we both were on the same wavelength as our desires, which brought them into fruition, and (b) we placed faith above fear. In other words, we didn't let fear get in our way or stop us from achieving our goals. This is how we were able to manifest our desired goal to be married — and to be married on the exact date of our choosing.

That's not to say fear wasn't present. When I was on the journey to manifest my husband, I felt the fear and the doubt, yes. Many of us do when we are using our magic to bring to us something that we haven't had before. Whether it's getting a book deal, starting a business from scratch, or leaving a comfortable job to launch a consulting firm, the most successful people have felt the fear and taken the leap anyway. They went forth in the unknown and came out successful on the other side.

When something scares you, know that it is simply your subconscious mind rising up and presenting you with the perception of failure. Failure to be a good parent when you have a baby on the way. Failure to motivate a crowd on your first public speaking venture. Failure to get promoted when you're up against a colleague. Failure to make a relationship work. *It is just a perception that hasn't happened.* When you are fearful, you are in a place where you are perceiving a situation will go wrong, rather than going *right*. But you can control your outcome by taking action to be prepared to overcome whatever it is that scares you.

Even though I wasn't really thinking about marriage at this time in my life, I found that I was excited about the possibility. The fear that I did have (we hadn't even talked about marriage at this point) was of rejection. *What if he would never propose? What if he didn't want to be married? What if we were on two different pages with nothing in common when it came to what we each wanted in life?* What worked for me to overcome fear was to nip those thoughts in the bud and choose faith instead. I enjoyed living my life every day; I stayed in the moment. Sometimes we get so caught up in thoughts of the future that we fail to live in the present. When I focused on being happy for how things were working out for me, more amazing things started to work out for me. Also, I know my worth. And because I knew that I was deserving of the essences I was calling in in a husband, I attracted him.

About nine months after my conversation with Richelle, my then boyfriend bought a house and asked me to move in with him. My lease was up at my condo, and I thought, *Why not? We're moving in the right direction.* Three months later, we were married, and three months after that, we whisked ourselves away to sunny California for his brand-new job and my brand-new life. My life had completely changed in the span of a year. I called Richelle from our new place in Los Angeles and caught her up on all that had happened to me. We couldn't believe how amazing our lives had turned out. We'd have weekly coffee chats over FaceTime and check in to see how the other was doing. At this time Richelle and her husband were venturing into property investments. A year later they started a successful business helping other people invest in real estate as well.

Now you might be saying, *That's great, but what if I've done stuff while scared and I still failed? What about that, Clo? Huh?* And I'll tell you that you probably didn't fully surrender to all the expectations that you've ever had of yourself. Meaning, there may be some areas of your life where you don't feel worthy of having something. Meaning, you still need to unblock in those areas to allow what you're calling in to come through. You have to put your trust in the Universe that it will bring you what you feel you're worthy of having *and* take the aligned actionable steps to manifest what you want in your life.

Let's get one thing straight: Choosing faith over fear does not mean doing reckless things and expecting amazing results. Choosing faith over fear does not mean walking out of your comfortable job right now without a plan B. Choosing faith over fear does not mean ignoring your daily responsibilities. It isn't that. Not at all. If you leave your nice, cushy job and expect to start a thriving business the next day with no idea what you're doing, bless yo' heart, but it probably won't work out for you. You have to put in the work, aka the *action*, in order to make your dream a living reality. The world we live in doesn't just work in our favor with the snap of our fingers. We *do* need money in this world to live. To pay our bills, to feed and clothe and shelter ourselves. To take care of our responsibilities. To explore and to have fun. To fund our dream. To just be. We also have to take action in this world in order for our magic to work. It isn't one without the other. Our magic within will work only once we have applied everything that I've taught you so far. Remember? It goes back to chapter 3:

Affirmation + Belief + Action = Higher Vibrational
Frequency

When we visualize and say what we want to bring into existence, we believe in it wholeheartedly, and we take *action*, that is how we raise our vibration to meet the vibration of the thing we want. *This is how our magic works, OK?*

Always remember, when you believe in something wholeheartedly, there is no room for fear, and that is why choosing faith over fear will always equal a fruitful life. Because faith is stronger than fear and will overrule it any day, anytime.

How to Know When Your Magic Is Working

You'll know that your magic is working when you find that small things are happening in your favor. They may even snowball into larger things. You may also feel a warmth in your core; that is a signal that your goals will soon become your reality.

Here are some signs that your manifestations are coming to life:

- You notice an improvement in your relationships with your friends, family, and co-workers.
- People seem drawn to you.
- You notice positive changes within yourself.
- Others notice a positive change about you.
- No one has power over your emotions except you. *(Bad days? What are those?)*
- You react positively to daily events.
- You don't get angry over things that would once have upset you.
- You're happy.
- Everything just seems to work out for you.

A client of mine recently told me that she felt as if she wasn't seeing progress in achieving her goal of opening a Pilates studio. She was stuck in one part of the process, and she didn't know how to move forward. After going through a divorce and losing her job and having to repair her credit, she wasn't sure how she'd ever start over again. She felt lost.

However, she was able to push past her fear and continue to take *action*. Just when things were looking rough, she received a call from a lender who had a special program for people like her. When she asked how he got her information, he said that her file was in his inbox — even though she hadn't sent it to him. She went through the approval process to get qualified for the loan, and in less than two months, she had secured her Pilates studio and was starting on the renovations.

What happened to my client was sheer magic. With her belief in opening up her Pilates studio, she never gave up and continued to take action even when it seemed like all the cards were stacked against her. Even though she thought she wasn't seeing progress, even though she was going through a rough time, failure wasn't her end result. She later mentioned to me that she had applied for several loans, and it was possible that her information had been passed on to the lender who was able to help her. Even when it seemed like all the cards were stacked against her, small synchronicities started happening, then snowballed into larger ones.

When you incorporate your magic into your everyday life *even when you don't feel like it*, you keep moving the needle a little further in your favor. Take action toward your goal. It can be something as simple as getting up in the morning before work to go to the gym or incorporating more green vegetables into your diet on a daily basis. Whatever it is, once you take those small steps that keep you moving in the direction of your goal, it is inevitable that you will find success. Just. Don't. Stop.

What to Do When Your Magic Isn't Working

When I was in my twenties, I was obsessed with money and the idea of looking and feeling rich. I would do anything in my power to make sure that my hair was always done and my nails matched my pedicure. I was always trying to keep up with the celebrities I saw on TV and look like I had my life together. Deep down inside, though, I was struggling. I couldn't pay my bills and even had trouble keeping gas in my car. One day, I checked my bank balance: it was $11.47. I cried in my empty two-bedroom, two-bathroom luxury apartment in Northville, Michigan, because I couldn't afford to furnish it. I didn't know how to get myself out of the hole I found myself in.

I could see that something in my life wasn't working. I didn't want to be just another Black girl who tried and failed, another statistic, end of story. I wanted to *be the change*. I soon realized that I needed to stop doing the things that were draining my bank account without creating a return on investment. No more nail appointments. I started doing my own hair. I stopped buying new clothes every weekend. I even stopped hanging out with my friends. Instead of spending $50 every Saturday at some new restaurant, I saved that money and watched it grow. I applied for a higher-paying job in a new company, and I left my old $7.50 per hour job behind. I started to make new friends who were in tune spiritually with themselves, and my entire life changed.

When we continue to do the same thing over and over again, expecting new results, we only get more of the same. When we take action, no matter how small, we drive change to work out in our favor. When we reach out for help — to others or to Spirit — we receive it.

If your magic isn't working, make sure you're applying all the tools that I've talked about in this book. Also, have patience with yourself. You are a masterpiece that is ever evolving. Greatness takes time. Remember that.

Prosperity Is a State of Magic

When you think in terms of being rich, you not only think about money, but you think about being prosperous as a whole. You can't drive your big, 'bout it Benz if you're sick, right? Not even if you're unhappy. What's the point of having the whole cake if you can't even eat it? Being prosperous in all areas of your life is crucial to living the life of your dreams.

When you're in a state of magic, your prosperity grows along with your inner knowing that the Universe, Source, and/or God (whatever you'd like to call it) is within you. When you live in a state of abundance, you live in a state of magic, where God and the Universe work hand in hand in your favor. Things always work out for the better; you achieve great success. Prosperity comes when you put your trust in a power greater than yourself and live with the inner knowing that everything will be just fine.

MAGIC ACTION

Designing the Year of You

In this exercise, I'm going to lead you through creating your own one-year goal, what I like to call the Year of You. Think of something you want to have accomplished one year from now. It can be anything. I want you to spend time focusing on visualizing your dream and feeling how it will feel to have it. You can do this anywhere that allows you to have a few quiet moments to yourself. As with all these exercises, make sure you're relaxed and comfortable. Let's begin.

1. Take a notebook and a pen and write down one goal you wish to accomplish in the next year. *I will be a real estate agent this time next year, selling million-dollar listings. I will move across the country to my dream town exactly one year from now.* Whatever you'd like.
2. Write down the exact date one year from now.
3. Read your note aloud and then silently to yourself.
4. Imagine your dream already being yours. A successful real estate agent. A new homeowner. A new business owner. A new millionaire. A successful author. The next senior director in your organization. The first female CEO of your company. Whatever the goal is, imagine it is happening now.
5. Feel how it will feel to achieve this goal. Play the scenario in your mind and get as detailed as possible. Will you celebrate your dream becoming your reality by going to a nice restaurant? Maybe take a spa day? Did I hear you say a trip to Aspen? All right now! Feel it. Sit in this feeling for as long as you can, until it begins to fade away.
6. Become the new you, now. How do you act? Are you more confident? Have you lost weight or toned up for

this new you? Become that person today. Act and think
as if you are already your future self.
7. Slowly come out of this feeling.

The more you practice this visualization, as well as taking
the necessary action steps to obtain it, the sooner it will become
yours.

Chapter 6

Rewriting Your Story with the Snap of Your Fingers

You can only become truly accomplished at
something you love. Don't make money your goal.
Instead, pursue the things you love doing, and then do
them so well that people can't take their eyes off you.

— MAYA ANGELOU, Pulitzer-Nominated American Author,
Presidential Medal of Freedom Recipient, Civil Rights Activist

As I mentioned in chapter 2, I grew up in Detroit, Michigan, off Dexter Avenue and Joy Road. For those who don't know, this was one of the roughest neighborhoods on the west side of Detroit. Now, just because I grew up in the hood doesn't mean I didn't have a great childhood. My grandmother (who I called Grumma) and mother bent over backward to make sure my brother and I had the best life possible.

And we did. Our childhoods were amazing.

My brother went to Japan when he was in the fifth grade so he could study Japanese for two weeks and immerse himself in a new culture. And I went to West Africa with my mom when I was ten years old so I could understand and learn about my ancestors. We didn't do too bad at all.

We did pretty all right.

But we also weren't rich.

And we lived in the hood.

You see, my grandmother and my grandfather bought their first home back in the 1950s. They were actually the first Black family to move into the neighborhood. But as Black people moved in, white people moved out and into the suburbs, driving the value of the homes in the neighborhood down and the value of the homes and land in Metro Detroit up.

Anyways.

There were times when I would overhear my family talk about money struggles, and it made me cognizant at a young age that money "didn't grow on trees." It also planted a seed in my mind: I assumed I would need to hustle in order to live the kind of life I wanted, because that's what most people around me did.

My daddy was a hustler. He left us when we were small kids. He tried to come back when I was sixteen, but by that time, there really wasn't much parenting for him to do. My mom and brother said no, but I, on the other hand, allowed my dad to be a part of my life. From the tender age of sixteen, I was introduced to gambling at the racetrack and hustlin' with my daddy on the weekends.

I realized pretty quickly that hustlin' wasn't a sustainable career. I wondered why my dad continued to bet on horses, taking chances, knowing that he could lose all his money in one bet and not have enough left over to put gas in his car, let alone pay his rent. But all in all, I was enamored of the stories he'd tell me about how he and my mom met and how he moved to Detroit from Savannah, Georgia, in the summer of '72 in search of a better life. I miss talking to my daddy. RIP.

Needless to say, I sometimes hung out with him at the track just to listen to him talk and try to soak in the missing ten years that he was out of my life. I also spent a lot of time dropping my daddy off at the track so I could drive his Cadillac and pretend I was *that girl* as I rode all round the city of Detroit.

Most times when I was driving the Caddy, I would think about how I could live my life driving a luxury car, living in a luxury house, and having the big bucks in the bank. Though my dad wasn't what I would consider wealthy, his image implied that he was. Besides driving a Cadillac, he was living in a five-bedroom mansion in Auburn Hills and portraying himself as a real estate investor.

My dad didn't own any of it.

The Cadillac belonged to a friend who allowed him to drive it and run errands on their behalf. My dad rented the house for a nominal fee until the owner could sell it. The real estate investing? My dad dibbled and dabbled, but it wasn't anything to write home about. I loved my dad dearly, but his way of living was that of a finesser. I, on the other hand, knew I wanted to live in a completely opposite way.

But when you're surrounded by the things you don't know how to get and people who don't know how you can get them either, it makes you believe that finessing may be the only way to achieve what you want. So, as time went on, my dad continued to finesse.

The one thing I can say about my daddy is that once he came back into my life, he came through for me and my mom whenever we needed him. Like when I turned seventeen and I wanted my first car. My dad saved up nine hundred dollars and bought me a red Grand Am. My favorite, favorite car of all time. Sure, the fact that it didn't have any heat wasn't great for the single-digit temperatures of the cruel Michigan winters, but that didn't stop me and my best friend, Jennifer, from driving to Eastland Mall to walk around and talk to boys. I had a car. Nothing else mattered.

But the moral of the story is, I knew I wanted more out of

life. For one, a car with heat in the winter so I wouldn't see my own breath as I drove all over town.

As time went on, my frustration grew. All my friends were from the hood. How was I ever to understand that I could use the power of my magic to transport me to the life I knew I was meant to live?

Let's fast-forward to present-day Chloe.

Out of the hood? Check.

Out of Detroit? Check.

You good? Check.

You great? Check.

But *how*?

I realized that I needed to remove myself from people and situations that weren't bettering my quality of life. Meaning, I needed to be around people who were at the place I wanted to be or at least ten to twenty steps ahead of me. When you spend time around people who emulate the success you want, it shows up in your life. New ideas come from nowhere. You get invited to events to meet other like-minded people. Your mind expands. Your way of thinking expands. You expand. Get it?

You can't get advice from someone who is in a backward position and expect it to transform your life. If someone's energy is draining you, you need to remove yourself from that person or protect your energy. In my case, when I was around those kinds of people, I protected myself by imagining I took my energy out of my body and placed it inside an imaginary box. This way, other people's influence had zero effect on me. When I would get back home, I'd take my energy out of the box and put it back on. As silly as it may sound, it worked. (Still works today.) I also studied the works of motivational experts like Earl Nightingale, Deepak Chopra, and others. These people inspired me with their words and showed me that I could have what I wanted in life. I just needed to start my journey to attract that life to me.

Back in my teenage years, my dad would preach to me about boys. "Don't let them touch you. Don't hang around them. Just stay *away.*" This from a man who had missed the last ten years of my life, though his advice was sound — he didn't want me to end up as a teenage statistic. He tried his best, but he couldn't help me in other areas of my life where there was lack. For example, he couldn't teach me financial sense or how to manage my money. He didn't know how to teach me about stocks, IRAs, hiring a money manager, or putting 10 percent of my paycheck away each payday instead of blowing it on cheap clothes from discount chains that littered the inner city. Living below my means. He didn't know, right?

So as much as I loved my dad and valued spending time with him, in the areas I sought growth, I had to look elsewhere.

How to Keep a Magically Inclined Mind

Your family and friends love you, but they may not always understand you. Your journey to prosperity and living the life of your dreams is not for them to understand. Your goals may sound impossible to them, like chasing impossible dreams among a sea of doubts. You have to be OK with them not knowing how you're going to accomplish all your goals and dreams. They may unintentionally sabotage them.

To keep my dreams alive and well, I've found it best to keep my goals and dreams close to my heart and to not disclose any information until they have already manifested. People you love can inadvertently (or not — some folks are petty like that) influence you with their talk of how hard times are for them and how broke they are. And though that may be the case *for them,* don't allow others to influence you with their negativity. Steer clear of them and the evil spells they speak. Words are magic, and writing is spell work. If you think about it constantly and speak it into existence, then that thing will eventually become your reality.

Another important tool for keeping your mind inclined toward magic is what I call thought energetics. There are two kinds — and you definitely want to know the difference!

Higher thought energetics, or HTEs, are when you think positive thoughts on a conscious level. This is when your magic, the Universe, and your Higher Self have an opportunity to expand through you. These positive thought energetics power and improve your life. *Lower thought energetics*, or LTEs, are thought patterns that create lack or blocks in your subconscious mind. These form inner walls against the higher energetics of your magic.

Obviously, HTEs are where you want to put your focus. Here's an example of a higher thought energetic:

I choose to live an abundant life.

Remember in chapter 1 we talked about the conscious and subconscious minds? The conscious mind is like the spotlight on what you're doing right now — reading this book. Your action is focused, deliberate, and at the forefront of your awareness. Now picture this: You've been reading this book regularly and applying its principles in your life. You find yourself becoming the person you've always wanted to be, and your manifestations are showing up in your life. That's your subconscious mind at work. This is the part of your mind that has stored all the knowledge you've learned from this book and now uses it without any deliberate action.

Prosperous Conscious Thinking = Prosperous Life

When you think mostly positive thoughts, you are consciously creating a higher experience for yourself, allowing abundance into your life. When you are easily influenced by negative thought patterns and belief systems and you focus on negative outcomes, you are filling your subconscious mind with blocks, making it difficult for you to create the life you want.

To change your reality, you must change your mind. When you find yourself surrounded by negativity, you have to pull yourself out by reminding yourself that you are the co-creator of your life and that you have the power to create happiness, prosperity, and peace within yourself. One single positive thought can obliviate a thousand negative ones. When you believe and speak your magic into existence, it becomes your reality.

Remember that you and your Authentic Self are one. When you go within by practicing meditation, you are going to Source. You are going to God, the All-That-Is, Infinite Intelligence, or whatever you'd like to call it. When you connect with your Source, you are eliminating negativity from your life and working at a much higher level.

MAGIC MOMENT

Everyday Superpower Affirmations

These affirmations will help you release negativity, blocks, and inner walls that your subconscious may have built up within you. There are a few ways you can work with these. Try selecting one affirmation that resonates for you and repeating it during your meditation session. Or get a piece of paper and a pen and write down your affirmation of choice, looking at it every so often when you can take a break or a moment to yourself during the day. Best of all, try repeating all these affirmations daily every morning for the next week.

- *Everything always works out for me.*
- *I am the source of abundance in my life.*

- *I face my fears and live the life of my dreams.*
- *Every day, I show up and continue to be the person I have dreamed I would always be.*
- *I am becoming. My life is ever evolving in my favor.*
- *Great things are happening to me. I am excited for my journey ahead.*
- *I am in perfect health. I am immune from disease and illness.*
- *I take excellent care of myself every single day.*
- *I am a prosperous being.*
- *God is in me. God and I are one.*
- *I am open and receptive to all the abundance in the Universe.*
- *My income increases constantly.*
- *I am an irresistible magnet for all that belongs to me by divine right.*
- *Infinite Spirit, open the way for great abundance to me.*

 ## GO EVEN DEEPER

Releasing old, negative thought patterns can take time. Bad habits die hard, as we all know, so I've created this Creative Imagining to help you break through the barriers that are keeping you stuck and playing small. You do deserve the life you want, but you have to believe it deep down inside more than anything. To get started, please go to my website to access your Creative Imagining audio: ChloePanta.co/um-3.

Chapter 7

The Universe Is Your Co-creator

You are the universe, expressing itself as a human
for a little while.

— ECKHART TOLLE, Spiritual Teacher,
Bestselling Author, Master Motivator

G od is not fire and brimstone. I don't know who needs to hear this, but that source of power does not exist. God is not going to punish you by throwing your body into a pit of fire with demons and dragons if you fail to obey or commit a sin.

I remember going to some random church with Grumma one day when this pastor talked of such. "And if you have sex before marriage, you're going to *hell*!" he said, looking straight at me. I gulped and slinked down in my seat. The church was small, and out of the ten people who were in the church, I was the only one under seventy — well, me and the pastor, who said he was a reclaimed drunk who'd found God, and who now felt the need to talk lowly to others. Anyway, needless to say, I did not go back to that church with Grumma after that day.

God or the Universe is the ever-encompassing light, full of love and compassion and dreams coming true. The Universe is your biggest cheerleader, cheering you on in your movie of life. The Universe doesn't punish you if you've done something "wrong" or "bad," whatever that is. You aren't going to go to hell for your sins, whatever they may be. You will, though, go through lessons and journeys that you will (hopefully) learn from, to become a better you and to avoid the mistakes you've made in the past. You live heaven and hell on this earth. They are your experiences — not some place you venture off to after your death. You also have the choice to create an amazing experience in this life and to craft the life of your dreams because, well, you deserve it.

The Universe lives within you. Whenever you need something, all you have to do is go within. When you use your magic to go into your core to connect with Source, you are deepening your connection with your Authentic Self, your power, and your ability to create a prosperous life.

I co-create the life I want. Not even the sky is the limit.

Taking Action Is Having Faith in Yourself

Thinking positively is great and all, but when you think *and* take aligned action toward your goals and dreams, you are moving in the right direction. As I've said before and will say again, taking action is a necessary component for creating the life you want to live. Sometimes it can feel scary and uncertain, but isn't it scarier to do nothing and live in Shoulda, Woulda, Coulda Land? Yeah, it is.

One reason it can feel scary is because there's that thought in the back of your mind that you might fail. And it's true, you might fail and fail again, but you always have the choice to get up and try again. Those of us who stay down are defeated. But when you choose faith over fear, you'll always win. That is the power of having faith.

Remember what we talked about in chapter 3?

Choosing faith over fear = a fruitful life

I'm going to keep reminding you throughout the book, because I don't want you to forget it. When you have faith in something you want, it means that you have eliminated self-doubt and uncertainty and you're ready to take action to make that thing your living reality. It means that you have faith in your True Self. You are worthy of having what you deserve.

Having Faith in Your True Self

Now you may be wondering, *What is my True Self? Aren't I true to myself already?* And the answer is: It depends.

You have two selves within you:

- *You have the temporary housing self.* This is the self that has been conditioned by society (suffering from inferiority complex, identity issues, self-worthlessness, etc.). This self usually has limiting beliefs, suffers from low self-confidence, has money problems, needs motivation, has insufficient appreciation, and is deficient in ideals and possibilities.
- *The other self is the real you.* This is the magic spark in your life, your inner magic that is the reason you exist. This is your Authentic Self, your True Self, and the ultimate flawless *you*. This is the you that pushes beyond boundaries, goes after what you want in life, dreams wild, dares to take action, and makes shit happen. This is the *real you*.

To make your dreams your living reality, you need to identify with the real you. Release any self-doubt, negativity, and fears. The world *does* need that special gift that you have deep down inside you, and you *can* make your dreams your living truth.

How to Co-create with the Universe

All of us are connected to our limitless power, our magic. Just as there is unlimited air to breathe, there is an unlimited amount of magic for you to tap into to create your lovely life. There is plenty to be had, and there will never be a shortage.

When we tap into our magic, we are tapping into a limitless flow of energy, a limitless source of power that can provide us with anything we desire beyond our wildest dreams. We become superhuman and use our superpowers to manifest easily and effortlessly the life that we so desire. I've realized that the more I meditate, focus on expansion, and stay in tune with my reality and the metaphysical world (*The what?* More on this in a moment), the happier I become and the more quickly I can manifest things I want into my life. Crazy, right? Yeah.

But it's real.

And it works.

So you may have asked, *Clo, what is the metaphysical world?*

The metaphysical is the world beyond. The invisible layer that you cannot see. This is the world that holds our dreams and co-creates with us to make them our living realities. Day by day, as you continue to step into your power, you will realize that you have a personal connection with and a companion in the Universe. By keeping yourself in tune with this relationship, you will begin to realize that you are not alone in this game called life. Rather, you are the co-creator of your very own life.

The Universe co-creates with you and will bring to you whatever you focus your attention on. Whether that's a good thing or not is totally up to you. Your co-creator will direct and guide you toward the things that you want when you are aligned with your True Self. When you are not aligned with your True Self and are acting out as your temporary housing self, the Universe will try to get you back on the right path by sending obstacles and challenges your way. This isn't the Universe punishing you, it is simply nudging you to get on the right path to becoming who you are meant to be. When you are in tune with your Higher Self and you know that there is a greater force beyond anything you can imagine working on your behalf, you become inspired to take action to change your life for the better.

How Meditation Encourages You to Generate Ideas

When you sit in silence in meditation, you are quieting your mind. The noise in the outside world becomes void, and it all becomes about your breath. With each inhalation, you are realizing that you are alive. With each exhalation, you are letting go.

During the meditative state, you are connecting with your Higher Self and the Universe. You are beginning the process of consciously co-creating your life. When the outside noise is temporarily muted during this state, innovative ideas are free to come to you. Have you ever been in a situation where you didn't have the answer to a problem? Meditation can open the channels to allow the answers to flow freely. Things begin to come to you. Sometimes seemingly out of nowhere. You just know what to do. When you have a consistent meditation practice, this can be the outcome. As innovative ideas flow, action grows and takes place. You are allowing abundance to flow freely into your life. This is why cultivating a consistent meditation practice is a key to success and growth.

Meditation has several purposes:

- To help you get comfortable with consistency.
- To stimulate your mind to encourage you to act on your dreams.
- To fill your mind with innovative ideas for you to apply.
- To allow the abundance, success, and happiness that come with applying actionable steps toward achieving your goals.

Action Guidelines for Success in Co-creating

When you meditate, keep in mind the following guidelines to help you create rapid success in your life:

- *What you think about becomes your reality.* Knowing this, focus your attention on the things you want to happen to you. Whenever an idea pops into your mind during meditation, know that it is a higher power at work bringing you closer to your dreams. Take action to bring your results to you more quickly.
- *The only thing holding you back from taking action is you.* Don't let excuses rule you. Plans change, life happens — I get it. But if you don't take action toward your goal, nobody else will do it for you. Make sure you are putting yourself first.
- *Your Higher Self has your back.* Know that when you do take action on an idea, it is your Higher Self (not your temporary housing self) at work, co-creating with you, bringing to you what it is that you want.

Your Attitude Reflects Who You Really Are

One night, a close friend and I went out to an upscale bar in Detroit to celebrate her birthday. As we entered the bar, three women cut in between us, one of them yelling, "Excuse me!" as she pushed past. But my friend reached the maître d' before they did, and they ended up waiting behind us, the woman mumbling things under her breath to her friends. Then she got louder and said that we were in the way of her and her friends, moving too slowly.

Now, this situation could be handled several ways, but regardless of the outcome, I knew the behavior of that woman had zero to do with me. I just ignored her and laughed and joked with my friend. That person doesn't exist in my orbit, so why should I give her the time of day? The satisfaction of saying something nasty in return does not make you the better man or woman — it means that person has the ability to get a response out of you and therefore to take hold of your power. Clapping back isn't always necessary. You don't have to do it at all. Remember that your reactions are a 100 percent reflection of who you really are. And when you behave in a manner that doesn't give the other person any power over you, well — *that's* when you're using your magic.

That said, I know that keeping a positive attitude may not always feel easy to do. Some days you're just not in the mood. Maybe you're going through a tough time, or you're unsure of your next step in life. Regardless of where you are right now, focus on having a positive attitude.

When I say "positive attitude," I'm talking about when you have a solid foundation of faith in something that you believe in. Maybe you want to start a podcast and you have no idea what to do. Regardless of what's happening right now, maintain a positive attitude by knowing that the right idea will come to you at the right time. When you believe in something with all your heart, it has no choice but to come true.

When you believe that your life will be amazing and that everything will always work out for you, it does. When you nurture a positive mental attitude, you are telling the Universe that you believe in the power of you and that you know the Universe is cocreating in your favor. When you have this inner knowing, things in your life will begin to shift for you.

Now that we know the importance of cultivating a positive attitude, let's talk about the negative side of things. A negative attitude is when you think negative thoughts about yourself and others. You may feel that nothing good ever happens to you or that in general you really aren't happy. You don't know what to do in life to get ahead, and you think negatively about others and complain. This attracts unfavorable things in your life.

Getting Off the Merry-Go-Round

Sometimes the lessons you're supposed to learn don't change your life because you don't take action. You may feel like you're looping through the same scenarios over and over again, and you don't know why or how to get off the merry-go-round. That could mean you remain unhappy because of a mental blockage preventing you from living the life you want. But don't worry, I'm going to show you how to change this. My technique called the Magical Magnetic Method can help you overcome negative thought patterns — aka your limiting beliefs — so that you can rewire your neuropathways (more on this later), eliminate these blockages, and live the life you want, starting right now.

But first, here's an important reminder:

Your ideas only work when you do.

That's right: these techniques only work if you do. Yes, work is required. Put in the work daily to reap the results. It's painless, I swear.

So here we go.

Magical Magnetic Method

- *You must want to change and to unblock the areas of your life that are keeping you stuck in your current state.* Identify the areas in your life where you're stuck, and actively seek opportunities for growth. If you want to truly break free from barriers, you must do courageous things. It starts with aligned action.
- *You must reprogram those areas with what you want to see in your life.* For example, if you've felt unworthy in the past because a parent or someone else told you you weren't good enough, you must do the inner work to come to know that

you are worthy and good enough for whatever you desire in this world. You must deeply and truly want to be happy and successful in your life (whatever that may look like to you) and take the necessary aligned Magic Action steps to get where you want to go.

- *You must 100 percent believe and have an inner knowing that the life you want, even though it isn't here yet, can and will be yours.* It already is yours. You just haven't yet arrived at that moment in time when you see it physically in your world.

I'll give you an example, because I know that was pretty deep. When I wrote my proposal for this book, I just knew that in this lifetime, I was going to be a published author. I felt it. I believed in it 100 percent. But besides my inner knowing and my feelings, I put in the work and took the necessary aligned Magic Action steps to get to where I am today. The same holds true for you. If you have a vision, that vision can become your reality *only* if you put in the time, energy, feelings, and aligned Magic Action steps to make that thing real. Otherwise, it will stay only a wish and a hope. This is a law of the Universe. Don't break the law.

Understood?

Let's carry on.

Limiting beliefs are not permanent. You have the magic within you to change your mind in order to change your reality. Know that when you are doing the work by using your magic, you are removing fears, blocks, and lower thought energetics (LTEs) so that you can create the life of your dreams. Remember we talked about LTEs in chapter 6? Forgot already? No problem. I got you. Lower thought energetics are thought patterns that create blocks in your subconscious mind — inner walls against the higher thought energetics (HTEs) of your magic. These are bad, and we don't want them in our lives. We want to eliminate them from our subconscious minds so we can focus on higher thought energetics.

It is important that you stay in tune with your higher thought energetics so that you can make and adopt positive choices to override negative choices. And in case you forgot about higher thought energetics (because sometimes you be forgettin'), this is what that means: higher thought energetics are what you generate when you think positive thoughts on a conscious level. This is when your magic, the Universe, and your Higher Self have an opportunity to expand through you because you've made the decision to be open and receptive to success. A higher power can go to work on your behalf to bring you what it is that you want in this life.

The table below gives you examples of what higher thought energetics are, what lower thought energetics are, and how to recognize them. My strong advice is to stick to the examples on the right and throw those LTEs on the left out of your life.

LTEs vs. HTEs	
Lower Thought Energetics (Negative — When You're on That BS)	*Higher Thought Energetics (Positive — Using Your Untapped Magic)*
Fear	Faith
Shame	Empathy
Doubt	Assurance
Confusion	Clarity
Failure	Success
Destruction	Self-control
Defeat	Renewal

Rewriting Your Neuropathways

Now you may have asked in the previous section, *What are neuropathways?* Here is the lowdown.

Neuropathways (also called neural pathways, which I will use interchangeably) are complex networks of our nerve cells in the brain and nervous system. These pathways are responsible for relaying information and enabling communication within the brain and among different parts of our nervous system. In other words, neuropathways are like passages or roads our brain uses to send messages from one part to the other. As an example, think of when you touch something hot and you burn yourself: a message goes through a neural pathway to your brain, quickly sending another message back to your hand to say, "Pull it away, yo!"

Your neuropathways can change and adapt. When you learn something new — like a skill for a job or how to manifest your dream life — your brain creates new neuropathways. It's building new passages or roads in your brain to handle the new information.

With consistency and aligned action, you can replace your old, limiting beliefs with empowering ones. This process is how your neural pathways are reshaped in your brain to align with the dream life you want to manifest, ultimately helping you to manifest your goals and transform your life.

When you decide you will focus on positive thoughts, make positive choices, and allow the Universe to eliminate any weaknesses and negative energies from your mind, you are using your magic and your higher power within to create success, joy, and fulfillment in your life. Using my Magical Magnetism Method, you can remove any weakness that is holding you back from your God-given power. You are magic.

You might be asking, *How do I use this method, and how is this all possible?* And I'll tell you that the magic of your mind is infinitely more powerful than any weakness in your mind. You truly can overcome anything once you put your mind to it.

Weaknesses are simply untrained thought patterns within the subconscious mind that come to your conscious mind in an attempt to control how you think and act. They are based on limited beliefs.

In other words, your weaknesses try to hinder your ability to succeed. Here's an example of how a pattern of thoughts — weaknesses based on limiting beliefs — might unfold:

- You're trying to lose weight, and you're struggling.
- You feel that you just aren't meant to be the size you want.
- You make excuses for not creating healthy habits or getting adequate exercise.
- You can't control yourself when you see sweets. You just have to have them.
- You always say, "Next time." It's always, "Next year. New you."

These thoughts are weaknesses keeping you stuck. You may even believe them to be true. You may feel that you can't go to a restaurant without ordering whatever you want; your excuse is that you're out. When you have no self-control and no restraint, you have a weakness. Weaknesses have altered the way you think and have taken control of what you do in this area of your life.

Let's take a look at another example. Say you're trying to get a better, higher-paying job, but you lack experience. You have been putting off getting a certification in your field that would help get you to your higher-paying role. You might feel like:

- They'll never hire you.
- You don't have time to study.
- Interviews make you nervous.
- It will take too long to get certified or cost too much money, and you don't see the point.

- You're too old or it's too late to change careers or get more education.

Your weaknesses have tricked you into believing all this to be true. Remember when I talked about changing careers in my own life for a higher-paying job with no experience? Yeah. No experience. If it happened for me, why can't it happen for you? And don't tell me that it's because you're too this or too that. I read an article about a ninety-year-old-woman who graduated college. If she can do it, there is absolute certainty that you can too. The workplace is becoming more inclusive by the day, and I don't think you should let those limiting beliefs cloud your judgment.

MAGIC MOMENT

Affirmations to Transform Your Reality

In order to overcome your weaknesses in any area of your life, there are things you need to do. Using the list below, repeat the following affirmations, both silently to yourself and aloud, at least once a day. I have them on my phone set up as a reminder so that when I wake up, they're the first thing I see. I say them silently and aloud as I walk into my bathroom to start my day and as I look at myself in the mirror. I encourage you to add these to your phone as well, or print them out and put them up someplace where you can see them daily to reinforce your new way of thinking.

- *I want to change and will unblock my mind in areas of my life where there is lack.*
- *I deeply and truly want to be successful in life and will re-program or replace my lack mentality with uplifting words*

that I hold as true for myself: I am worthy, I am deserving, I am safe, etc.

- *I have an inner knowing that the life I want, even though it isn't here yet, can and will be mine. It already is mine.*

After you use these affirmations, the final step is to take *action*. No matter how big or small. Action is the key to overcoming weaknesses, achieving your goals, and living the life you want to live.

Chapter 8

Tapping into Your Power

When one door of happiness closes, another opens,
but often we look so long at the closed door that we
do not see the one that has been opened for us.

— HELEN KELLER, Author, Political Activist,
Overcomer of Obstacles Extraordinaire

It was 2008. At this point in my life, I was still confused about how things we think about become our reality. When people seemingly created miraculous things in their lives, I would stare at them perplexed, wondering, *How did they do that?* I knew I wanted to live an extraordinary life. I craved peace of mind, security, safety, and a feeling of holistic well-being. I just didn't know how to make those desires my reality. Take, for instance, one of my old friends. She was the Queen of Schemes. Whenever we'd discuss the topic of men, she'd say to me, "They play us all the time, so I play them."

She lived in the hood, but the house was paid for by one of her baller boyfriends. She didn't pay rent, and the car she drove, a brand-new Benz, was paid for by another baller friend.

Yet *another* baller boyfriend gave her a weekly allowance. Now, what did she do to receive these things? I'd rather not mention.

"What if he decides to take the car back?" I said one day when we met for dinner. I admired her Gucci outfit and her Cartier bracelet. She was fly, and I was curious as to how she managed to juggle three men without getting caught up.

"I know stuff about him that would put him away for a long time." She leaned in closer to me from across the table, speaking barely above a whisper. She smelled of Flowerbomb. "Trust me when I say he ain't stupid." She leaned back and picked up her French martini.

I often wondered why her way of thinking worked for her, even though in my mind it was dangerous. If any of these men decided he was done with her, he could take away her house, allowance, or car. Then what? She didn't have a job. To my knowledge she didn't have any skills. She grew up in the hood, so she did what she knew best. She was simply a finesser.

"But what if it did happen though?" I pressed the question, wondering if she had a plan B.

"Then I'll just find another one." She took a sip of her drink and smiled. "I know what I'm doing, Clo. Look at you, all worried about me and shit. I'm good."

Her game plan was simple. If she needed to replace a man, she'd ride around the side of town where the ballers could be found. She'd dress up to the nines, fake lashes, wig, and all. She was tall and slim and had a killer smile that could melt any man's heart. She'd sit at the bar of the five-star restaurant of her choice and wait until a victim fell prey. That was her game, and it worked like a charm — until it didn't.

After some time, my old friend and I fell out because I knew this wasn't the type of company I wanted to keep. The last time we spoke, apparently one of the baller boyfriends had taken the Benz. She wanted me to drive her to his house and help her steal the car back. *Hell naw. You must be*

Out.

Yo.

Mind.

Some years later, while driving through downtown Detroit, I saw her, and she saw me, and her mouth dropped. She tried to turn away from my view as she walked toward the bus stop with a baby in tow. No car. Catching the bus. So unlike the friend I knew from before who drove a brand-new Benz SUV.

It didn't surprise me. Not one bit. Her game eventually caught up with her, and she didn't seem like the baller finesser she once was.

I remember one night she had told me that all men cheat. That was her belief. She said that every man had cheated on her mother and her grandmother and her, so she had no faith that any man would be loyal to her. Because she thought like that, she also cheated men. She thought that by cheating others, she would live a better life than she could on her own. You don't have to cheat others in this world to live a good life. You can live by morals and values and create an amazing, abundant life. Unfortunately for my old friend, she was genuinely unhappy. Though at the time I didn't know it, she wanted an honest life, she just didn't know how to get there.

Moral of the story is, what we believe to be true for us will be. She believed men were natural cheaters, always up to no good, and that's how her baller boyfriends turned out to be. They eventually decided they wanted their Benz and their house back — to pass down to the next girlfriend. Whatever the case, you don't have to focus on using other people. Instead, focus on doing good for yourself to get ahead.

When you surround yourself with toxic people in toxic environments, you can become influenced by their decisions and their way of thinking. You're actually surrounding yourself with LTEs, which lowers your own vibrational frequency level. This is a no-no.

The best way to rid yourself of toxic people is to stop hanging around them! The one thing we can never change is other people. We are all born with free will and the ability to make our own decisions. And as much as I felt afraid for my friend and the way she was living her life, no matter what I did or said to try to help her, it was 100 percent up to her to change her life. So instead of continuing our friendship, I ended it, knowing I didn't want that type of energy in my life.

When you eliminate toxicity from your life, you also eliminate toxic situations. You are saying to the Universe, "I want and deserve better than this. I am ready for and worthy of high-quality friendships." No one can coerce you into going somewhere or doing something with them that may cause you harm or, worse, cause other people harm. Don't put yourself in a situation where you are pulled into someone else's crisis. You can't save the world, but you can save yourself.

If you ever find yourself in a sticky situation and you aren't sure how to navigate it, here is a technique that I've shared with my clients.

If someone is trying to force you to make a decision right away without time to think, you probably shouldn't make that decision right then and there. If you feel an urgency that a decision must be made now and you're not ready to, take a step back and hold off. You don't have to make rash decisions that you may later on regret. Take the time to think things through before jumping to decisions that can cost you. The Universe will always guide you to take aligned action with a sense of knowing or a positive feeling in your gut — not a sense of urgency to act rashly.

You have all the power anyway, but when a toxic person sees the opportunity to take advantage of you, they will. So it's best to keep the toxic folks out of your life. If you find it difficult to eliminate these people completely — maybe they're family members or someone close to you — take the necessary action steps to protect your energy and your peace.

If you find yourself slipping into a dark place, lift yourself up out of darkness and step into the light. Only you can save yourself. And you have the power to do so. Ask and it shall be given unto you. Never give your power away to anyone and leave your life up to chance. You are the captain of your ship. The pilot of your plane. The author of your story. The main character in your movie of life. *You* are. Why would you want to give your God-given gift away?

Those are some broad strokes for keeping yourself safe. Now, let's look in more detail at ways to remove toxicity from your life, so you can learn to take your power back once and for all.

Tips to Remove Toxic Relationships from Your Life

- *Let the other person know how you feel.* Nine times out of ten, if you haven't communicated to the person that you're unhappy in the relationship and that you want to cut ties, they probably don't know. Be clear and honest; tell them how you feel and that it's best to go your separate ways. Let them know in a calm manner, and don't stoop down to their level if they react irrationally. Remember that woman who cut in front of me and my friend in the upscale Detroit bar? This is why you're letting go.
- *Set hard boundaries — and mean them.* If you really want someone gone from your life, you can't tether yourself to the idea that they're gonna change and everything will be all right. If it's been the same toxicity for years, nothing will change them unless they decide to do it. Until that time comes (if ever), set hard boundaries and mean them. Don't respond to their emails, texts, calls, or social media DMs. If you're done, then be done. Make sure you don't give your power away.
- *Block them.* This one is quite easy. You block them from your life. You block their contact info and then you delete them, never to be seen or heard from again. You have the power here. Don't let a pessimistic person tell you otherwise.

If it's someone you can't fully block (maybe they're a family member or a co-worker), protect yourself emotionally. You do this by leaving your energy at the door before you interact with the person. What I have done, and what has worked like a charm for many of my clients and friends, is to pretend I am taking my energy out of my body before I make contact with the toxic person. Remember how I described this in chapter 6? Put your energy into an imaginary box and lock it. When you come back from being around the toxic person, you say the following mantra: *I release any negative energy that doesn't belong to me. I remove any negativity from my body. I am loved. I am safe. I am protected.* Now, unlock your box and put your energy back on. When you protect your aura and your energy, you are no longer permitting the toxic person's negative energy to latch on to your energy and alter your mood. You are allowing the toxic person's energy to move past you but not to stick to you.

- *Protect your energy with affirmations.* Another protective mechanism that I use is to tell myself that *I am safe. I am protected. I am secure.* This reassures me that my energy is protected, and no one has power over me and my decisions. *I am strong. I am worthy. I am protected.* These mantras have helped me block toxic people from my space and go on to live a healthy, happy, and amazing life. I wish the same for you if you are in this type of situation.

- *Spend more time with positive folks.* Surround yourself with people who do good and want to see you do good. They are out there, trust me. Those are your biggest cheerleaders. They cheer in your success and your happiness. You need more of those people in your life, people who accept you exactly as you are.

- *Talk to a professional.* Talking to someone can always help. Whether this is a life coach or a trusted therapist, talking to someone can help you work through any deeper issues at hand and sever ties with the toxic person or people in your life. They can also give you the support you need to cope with moving on from the relationship.

- *Forgive, even if you don't forget.* Forgiving someone who has harmed you is an act of love. It is the first step to letting go and moving on, the first step to healing. When you hang on to thoughts of those who wronged you, that anger sits deep within you, and you fester in those thoughts. This can cause disease and illness, not to mention sap you of your peace of mind. Release those negative thoughts and that anger by doing the Magic Action below. This will help you to forgive the person who has done you wrong. Even if you don't forget about what they did, you'll stop feeding it any of your power, as you're stronger than that now.

MAGIC ACTION

Negativity Detox

In this exercise, we will walk through how you can release your thoughts and feelings of negativity toward someone who has wronged you and forgive that person. I'd like you to get somewhere quiet and comfortable for the next few minutes as we complete this exercise.

1. With your eyes closed, place one hand on your heart and the other on your navel. Imagine in front of you is the person who has wronged you. If it is too difficult to imagine them, imagine a symbol that represents them. This can be an object, such as a water bottle or a piece of paper. Anything you can think of.

2. Next, I want you to imagine that you are talking to that person (or the object) and telling them how you feel.

How they have hurt you. Imagine them being passive and not showing any emotion. They cannot harm you and will not harm you during this exercise. They have no power over you.

3. Now I want you to say these words aloud or in your mind: *I release you. I release all negativity and toxicity that you brought into my life. You have no power over me, and you cannot hurt me. I release you and everything that you have done to me. I forgive you, and you can no longer hurt me.*

4. Next, imagine the person fading away, literally disappearing from your life. If you're representing them with an object, such as a piece of paper, imagine the piece of paper being shredded and then burning and disappearing into thin air. Whatever object you thought of, imagine it disappearing in thin air, out of your life.

5. To go even deeper into forgiveness, imagine sending love and light to that person. Imagine a heart coming from your heart and direct it to them. Wish them well and then close the chapter to this experience in your life. You have learned your lesson, and there is no going back.

You may be surprised that I suggested you send love and light to the person who wronged you. In chapter 10 I will explain in more detail why it is so important to not hold grudges and to send love and light to even the most toxic people. For now, just know that you have released this toxic person from your life spiritually and emotionally, and they cannot cause you any harm. Make sure you have also followed the "Tips to Remove Toxic Relationships from Your Life" earlier in this chapter, so that you have no contact with that person going forward.

Chapter 9

Manifestation Mastery

Just try new things. Don't be afraid.
Step out of your comfort zones and soar. All right?

— MICHELLE OBAMA, First African American First Lady
of the United States, *New York Times* Bestselling Author,
Advocate for Education and Health

When I first started consulting, I was introduced to getting comfortable with being uncomfortable. I just knew that I had to do something different, and I had to make it work. At this point, my husband and I had just moved to Los Angeles. I'd left my cushy job back in Michigan, and my young coaching business wasn't quite where it needed to be for me to do it full-time. So I took up a new skill and dived into the deep end of HR tech consulting. I had a goal and a plan: *We need more money in this expensive-ass city, and I need to make more money, fast.* In the early days, I worked on a project in San Francisco, and although it was extremely terrifying for me and gave me anxiety every night, it was equally satisfying. I lived in San Francisco during the week, and he lived in our apartment in LA. During the weekends, we'd meet in the middle, or he'd come to the Bay Area, or I'd go back to LA. Long story short, it was one of the best *and* scariest times of my life.

You know the saying "Fake it until you make it"? Yeah? Well, that was me during my six-month project in San Francisco. During the workweek I was Chloe the Consultant, and I recorded every meeting so I could replay it over and over again until I grasped every detail that somehow I had not understood in person. Over time, as I got better at what I did, my anxiety went away. And though pretending to be an HR tech consultant wasn't what I thought it would be, it did teach me that I really can do anything.

I overcame my fear of speaking in front of people. Presenting. Being assertive when I needed to be. I learned how to configure the back end of an HR system. From scratch. Of course, my husband helped me (he's a tech genius, by the way). And he always cheered me on and coached me after every workday. From that point on, with my consulting business, we were able to pay off our credit card debt, save, and feel comfortable in one of the most expensive cities in the world. As time went on, I pivoted from consulting back to coaching, but with my consulting knowledge, I was able to amass a hefty salary doing something I learned how to do on the job.

Now, I am not saying go out and apply to be a surgeon if you have no medical experience — absolutely not. But with the HR skills I already had, paired with learning the technology side of things, I was able to broaden my portfolio of knowledge to help me earn the income I wanted to earn. The moral of this story is that I was scared and did it anyway. What was the worst that could happen? I could get kicked off the project and learn more skills and find another project. Knowing that made me feel invincible, because I would keep on trying until I succeeded. And I did.

If you want to see a change in your life, whether that's more money, more peace of mind, or whatever, you first have to stop and be grateful for what you already have. When we mope around and complain and think all day long about what we *don't* have ... well, guess what? More of that lack will appear in our lives.

When we want to up-level our lives and manifest big, amazing goals and dreams, we not only have to think and act as if we already have those things, we have to *believe* that they are already ours, even though we can't see them yet.

For example, before I got my consulting gig in San Francisco, I pictured how I would act, what I would do, what I would wear, how people would perceive me. And then I became that person. I became Chloe the Consultant. I had to ask myself, *Who is Chloe the Consultant, and how does she act? What does she do? Where does she live?* I wrote down all those details, and I mapped them out.

How does Chloe the Consultant act?
She's determined, fierce, and about dat business.
What does she do?
She's a techno-functional HR consultant.
Where does she live?
In the East Bay, baby!

Now you might be asking, *Why is this important?* When we write down and visualize our goals and dreams, they become real for us. We can see ourselves acting out the part in our very own movie, starring us.

So, for me, I had to first visualize myself as Chloe the Consultant, and then I became her during my time in San Francisco. I knew that as a high-powered consultant, I wanted to live in the Bay Area, because some of the most successful people live in the East Bay in multimillion-dollar homes. I wanted to be a part of that vibe, so I pictured myself in it.

For you, let's do this same exercise, so you can also become the you that you want to be. Ask yourself the following questions. Get a piece of paper and a pen, and write down the answers.

- Who do you want to become?
- What are you being called to do?
- What are your core values?
- What are your strengths and weaknesses?
- How can you strengthen your weaknesses?
- What are your short-term goals and long-term goals?
- What does success look like to you?
- What fears or limiting beliefs are holding you back?
- How do you act?
- How do others perceive you?
- Where do you live?

As you write down your answers, be as vivid and clear with detail as you can. Don't just say in response to the first question, *I wanna be me.* We know that, but who are you, *really*? If your goal is to play in the NBA, who do you want to play like? Jordan or James? Be specific. If your goal is to be the next senior-level executive in your company, who do you want to be like? Thasunda Brown Duckett or Rosalind G. Brewer? Again, be specific. I use examples of successful people to help you imagine who you want to emulate. It could be your cool-ass aunt, for all I know, but it needs to be someone who you perceive as successful.

For the second question, don't think about what you should be doing — focus on what you feel your Authentic Self is calling you to do. Is that helping other people? Writing? Creating in some form? Focus on what lights you up, what you are being called to do in this world.

Continue writing down your other answers in this manner, digging deep inside to be as detailed and specific as you can in your visualizations.

How to Manifest Larger Goals into Your Living Reality

Manifesting big goals may seem scary. If you're trying to manifest optimal health and fitness and you don't even know where to start, you may feel that it's far from your reach. You may also feel that great big things only happen to other folks, not you.

When you're thinking of bringing the ultimate goal into your life, there are several things to consider. First you have to ask yourself, are you already taking the necessary actionable steps to reach that goal? Buying a big house ain't cheap, and just thinking about it all day long isn't going to bring it any closer to you.

You need to analyze your current situation and, as I've said before, feel grateful for where you are right now. That raises your vibrational frequency level to match that of the thing you want (your big ol' house), and it also tells the Universe, "Bring me more of the good stuff!"

When you mope around complaining, thinking about all the bills you have to pay and all the money you don't have, well, guess what? You're telling the Universe, "Bring me less money, more bills, and more things to complain about." Unfortunately, this is why some people, no matter how many years have gone by, are still stuck in the same routine, same situations, day after day, year after year. You're better than that, right? That's why you're reading this book, to change your life for the better.

The second thing you need to do is take the necessary steps to achieve the goal. If you want that house, does your income match it? If it doesn't, do you need to get a higher-paying job or start a side hustle? If you are already financially set, do you need to speak to a real estate agent to help you find your dream home? These are steps that are required if you're thinking of buying that dream home.

Sometimes we may feel unworthy of even having a goal. We may feel that we don't have the means to buy a home — or anything for that matter. Sometimes we can feel that we've struggled most of our lives — why should this be any different? I hear you. I've been there too, but I'm here to tell you that struggling is just a state of mind. When you change your mind, you change your life.

A single friend of mine from Detroit had dreams of becoming a homeowner. She thought that once she found her soulmate, they'd buy a house together and start a family. Years went by, and she hadn't met her match, but she was ready to buy a home. Though all those years she'd thought she needed to have a partner to achieve her goal of homeownership, she realized she was ready to achieve that goal now. Even though she didn't have a lot of money saved away, she qualified for a first-time homebuyer program and bought her first home with very little money down. What she had saved up was all she needed. She didn't have to find a partner to buy her home with, and she's now living in her dream house, whereas before she thought she couldn't afford to without the help of a partner.

Once you've taken the necessary steps to get closer to your goal, the third thing you need to do is have faith and believe that your goal will happen. Don't worry about how it will happen — leave that up to a power greater than yourself — but have an inner knowing that the work you put in will pay off.

Take Anise, for instance. She struggled for years with her coaching business. She worked as a teacher during the day, and her goal was to become a full-time life coach. As a single mom with two young kids, she didn't know how she could just up and quit her job and become successful as a coach. As the months went by, she put coaching on the back burner and decided that maybe she was just meant to be a high school English teacher.

One day after school, one of her students came up to her and said, "Ms. Johnson, can I ask if you could tutor me after school? I feel like I'm struggling, and I need help."

"Of course," she said. "I'd be happy to."

After several weeks of tutoring, her student became one of the top students in her class, and his mother came by to deliver her flowers to thank her. During their conversation, the mother said that her consulting firm was looking for an executive life coach and asked if she happened to know anyone. Anise mentioned her training as a life coach and how she'd love to be considered, as she wanted to transition from teaching to coaching. In a short time frame, Anise became an executive life coach, coaching C-level executives in corporations, and left her teaching job behind. She now makes more money than she ever dreamed of and does speaking engagements across the country. She's doing amazingly well.

I believe in the magic of the Universe,
for it is where dreams are born.

The point I'm trying to make here is that you have to be OK with not knowing how your dream will happen. Anise had pretty much given up all hope, but the Universe had other plans. Things may not always work out for us the way we think they will. Anise originally thought she'd be a life coach coaching her peers, not C-level executives. Her dream came to be something greater than she asked for initially. The Universe knows what you want; it hears you. Always know that when you ask for something, you may get what you asked for in a different form. It may come to you in an even greater form than you could have imagined. It will never be less than what you've asked for.

MAGIC ACTION

Manifesting Big, 'Bout It Goals

Here's the method for manifesting big goals into your living reality.

1. *Decide what you want and play around with it, try it on.*
   Want that big ol' house? Where is it? Who lives with you? How much is the mortgage? Interest rate? How

many bedrooms, bathrooms? Who's going to clean it? Imagine yourself there, walking around, living your life. How does it feel? These are the questions you need to seriously ask yourself and play around with. Does it feel too scary? That's OK. Try imagining a smaller goal, get comfortable with that, and then ask for increasingly bigger things until the really big goal feels just right.

2. *Take action, yo.* Remember, you need to actually do the work for your dream to come true. Earl Nightingale once said, "It's like the man who stands in front of the stove and says to it: 'Give me heat and then I'll add the wood.' How many men and women do you know, or do you suppose there are today, who take the same attitude towards life? There are millions. We've got to put the fuel in before we can expect heat." Same principle is at work here. Take the necessary action steps to get you closer to your goal. When you put in the work, you reap the rewards of life.

   Now, for some people, taking steps toward their goals may feel daunting. Does taking action steps make you feel anxious? I get it. Take small, bite-size steps so that it doesn't feel so scary. If your goal is to drop ten pounds to prepare for summer, maybe that's cutting four pounds a month for two and a half months. Your action could be exercising three to four days a week by doing strength-training exercises at the gym or hitting the trail to put in an hour-long walk. It could be filling only half your plate with starchy veggies and the other half with low-cal, non-starchy veggies. Whatever your goal is, the steps don't have to be big or scary or hard. You go at your own pace, as long as you keep it moving.

3. *Have faith in a power greater than yourself.* When you have an inner knowing that what you've asked for is

coming to you, it *is* coming to you. When my husband and I put in the offer on our sunny California home, I knew it was already ours. How? I put my faith in a power greater than myself. I knew we had done the work. I had the faith, and I surrendered. I wasn't needy or clingy. Sometimes you have to let things go, and if they come back to you, they are truly yours. When you go within yourself and put faith in something you cannot see, you have an inner knowing that everything is going to work out for you, and it will. Whatever your goal is, when you put in the work, you're consistent, and you put faith in the Universe to bring it to you, how can it not be yours?

Now you may be thinking, *What if I do all that and it still doesn't work?* And I'll tell you that what you've asked for is still a work in progress and something greater is on its way. Remember, our vibrational frequency must match that of the thing we are asking for. We have to be unblocked to accept what it is we're calling in. If we are still blocked in certain areas in our lives, we need to do the inner work to see our manifestation come to life. If your vibe doesn't match, then it won't come to you — yet. It will take time to get there. But as long as you believe and put in the work to raise your vibrational frequency, know that it's coming your way.

PART 3

How to Use Your

INNER MAGIC

to Change Your Life

Chapter 10

Sending Love and Light Out into the World

When you put love out in the world it travels, and it can touch people and reach people in ways that we never even expected.

— LAVERNE COX, Emmy-Nominated Actress and Emmy-Winning
Producer, LGBT Advocate, Boss Babe Extraordinaire

M y brother is one of the coolest people I know. He was the cool kid in high school, he's the cool dad to his kids, and he's the best big little brother a sister could ask for. I call him "my big little brother" because next to my five-foot eight-inch frame, he stands over six feet tall and has always been protective of me.

When we were kids, we didn't get along. We'd fight over just about everything. He had more freedom than I did growing up "because he's a boy," my mom always said. And I envied how he could stay out longer, do things I couldn't do, and go places I couldn't go, all because of that — even though he's two years younger than me. Can you believe that? But as we've grown up, the man he has become amazes me each and every day. I mean, to grow up off Dexter Avenue and Joy Road and to have a son who's not only a straight-A student in high school but a star basketball player at that? Come on! Who raised this kid? My brother did.

Every year, my brother contributes turkeys to families in need on Thanksgiving Day so they can have a happy Thanksgiving. Every year, my brother gives away backpacks full of school supplies for kids in need in Detroit so that they can have the tools to be successful. Every year, my brother donates thousands of dollars of his money to others, expecting zero in return. Every year, my brother throws a spectacular Christmas Eve party for all his friends and our family, with catered food and plenty of drinks to go around and a karaoke machine that plays anything you can rap to, from Street Lord'z to Jeezy. When the clock strikes midnight, he throws one thousand dollars in ones from his upstairs balcony so that the kids can collect the cash — some adults do, too. Last time, I collected eight dollars minus the one dollar some kid stole from underneath my grip. And he does this with love, not expecting anything in return. Sometimes it's hard to believe that a little boy from one of the roughest neighborhoods on the west side of Detroit grew into a man who has transformed his life for the better.

I'm proud of you, bro. And I love you.

When we give generously and expect zero in return, we reap the benefits. My brother is wildly successful, and I know it's because he gives freely. He wants to see everybody doing good, and he wants everybody to be happy, and because of that, he has been rewarded tremendously.

When I give to others, I am giving to myself.

When we give freely without expecting anything back, we're telling the Universe, *I have plenty, I am abundant, I am fearless*, and the Universe will give us more of that in return. We'll get more money, more prosperity, more financial security, because we know the Universe is looking out for us even if we can't see it just yet. Ever wonder why Oprah keeps giving stuff away? She's spent millions upon millions of dollars on gifts for random strangers all across the globe, and yet she is still one of the wealthiest women in the world. A billionaire, and her wealth continues to grow year after year. Have you ever thought about that? Why do people who give away so much always seem to have an overflowing cup? It is because they are in flow with the Universe and their vibration is so high that the Universe showers them with unlimited amounts of abundance. It's time to get in flow, folks. This is where you want to be.

On the other hand, when we give and expect something back, we aren't truly giving — we're being selfish.

When we're in a fear-based mindset, we hold on to what we have. We don't give, we don't share, we don't trust. We keep our scraps to ourselves because we fear there isn't enough to go around. And when we live like that, we are living in the LTE state of mind. Lower thought energetics keep us stuck, keep us broke, and keep repelling us from the things we want. We have got to rise above this level of thinking if we truly desire to be prosperous.

Be a Beacon of Love and Light

A friend of mine was in a really bad relationship. Her partner would do terrible things to her mentally, physically, and emotionally. After some time, she finally got out of that relationship, and she didn't date for quite a while, too shaken from what she had gone through.

She came to me one day and said, "Chloe, I just don't think I can trust anyone anymore. I've been through so much that I am afraid the next man will be him all over again."

I resonated with that — and I gave her an unorthodox suggestion. "As crazy as this may sound," I told her, "you have to send love and light out to him and let him go. You're still tied to him if you can't move on and live your life."

She looked confused as she thought about this deeply. "I just don't know how."

A lot of people don't know how. That's why I'm telling you in this book that even if someone did something unspeakable to you or to someone you know, if you hold on to your anger, you are only hurting yourself. Though it may be the most difficult thing to do, sending love and positivity to someone who has scarred you will actually be the most renewing thing you've ever done as weight falls off your shoulders. When we hold on to anger, we are giving other people power over us. To get our power back, we have to let go of the pain and the hurt and the fear from the past and live in the moment, starting today.

My friend spent years of her life hating a man who had wronged her. In those years, she passed up multiple opportunities to make a fresh, new start because she feared that the next man would be just like the last. Unknowingly, she was giving her power away to the previous relationship by not moving on from it. Once I showed her my technique for sending light and love into the world and letting go of past hurt (you'll learn this technique at the end of this chapter), she was able to move on and find love again.

This technique works only if you are truly ready to move on in your life, close a previous chapter, and forgive the person who has hurt you. This is giving at its finest, because you are sending your love and light to someone who probably at this moment in time doesn't deserve it.

So why give it then? you may ask. You give love away and you give light to others so that you, in return, will receive love and light — and what I mean by "light" is prosperity, abundance, happiness. You are cutting ties with this person, and you're going your separate ways. Forever. You are eliminating the hurt, the pain, and the fear. You are stepping out on faith and becoming the person you didn't know you could be — someone who forgives someone who hurt you beyond hurt.

I know, I understand.

I've been there.

And maybe you need to work on forgiving someone who has hurt someone you love, and you're struggling with that. Forgiveness is a complex process. It can be difficult to think of giving someone a free pass by forgiving them, especially if you're feeling angry, betrayed, and hurt. But ultimately, forgiveness is all about you. You have to release your negative emotions toward others so that these feelings don't fester inside you. Bottled-up negative feelings can result in turmoil, disease, illness, and overall unhappiness in our lives.

If you're struggling with forgiving someone who you feel doesn't deserve to be forgiven, the modalities I'm about to share are for you. At the end of this chapter, I'll teach you a Magic Action that will transform your energetic vibration into pure love and light. But first, let's walk through some tips to help you release all that pent-up negative energy that is causing you more harm than good.

Tips to Release Negative Energy toward
Those Who Have Harmed You

- *Acknowledge the feelings.* It's OK to feel angry, upset, betrayed, and hurt. Recognize and accept these feelings — but don't sit in them. Let them flow by like leaves floating through a stream. Don't let them fester inside you. Acknowledge them and then move on by letting them go.
- *Understand the circumstances.* Do you know the full story or only one side of it? Try to understand the situation from the other person's point of view. This by no means excuses their

actions, but it gives you perspective to help you understand their intentions.

- *Communicate.* If you're able to communicate in a way that is not triggering, let the person know how you feel and how the situation has affected you. This may also help you release negative emotions you are holding on to.
- *Practice empathy.* Use the Magic Action Love and Light Technique below to help you release pent-up energy and remove negative emotions from your body, replacing them with healing empathy.
- *Release and let go.* You've done the work. Now it's time to go out and live your life, closing this chapter and leaving it behind.

MAGIC ACTION

The Love and Light Technique

It may feel like it will take every fiber of your being to say the mantra I'm about to give you, but I promise you, once you say these words, there's no going back.

You will be renewed.

You will be healed.

You will live a much better, happier, healthier, and more abundant life than you ever thought possible.

But you must do the work, and you have to give freely, because that's how this thing works. So. You ready? Let's go.

1. Get into a quiet space and close your eyes. Place one hand over your heart and the other on your navel. Take a deep inhalation and say, *I Am.* On your out breath, release any negative thoughts and feelings. Send them out into the air, no longer holding on to them, no longer making them a factor in your life.

2. Repeat this step three times, going deeper each time.
3. When you get into a meditative state, say the following mantra: *I send love and light out into the world to heal all those who have hurt me. I send love and light out into the world to all those who are in pain, to all those in need, and to all those who know not what they do. I send love and light to heal the world, and I send love and light to all those who wronged me. And as I do so, I in turn heal myself. I will not let others' past doings affect me or any other person who is brought into my life. For I deserve happiness, abundance, and a life full of prosperity. It is my divine right, and so it is. I am worthy.*

✦ GO EVEN DEEPER ✦

I know that forgiving others can be tough — especially if we've experienced unthinkable abuse and are struggling to find peace in our lives. I've created something special just to help you dive even deeper into the Love and Light Technique and rewire your way of thinking, forgive those who hurt you, and move past the hurt. Please go to my website to access your Creative Imagining audio: ChloePanta.co/um-4.

Chapter 11

Forgive, Even If You Don't Forget

The weak can never forgive.
Forgiveness is the attribute of the strong.

— MAHATMA GANDHI, Indian Revolutionary, Leader of the
Non-violent Resistance Movement, Political Ethicist

In 2008, it was a Hot Girl Summer for me. I had just lost
about thirty pounds, was newly single, and was living it up.
My friends and I would ride around downtown Detroit, giving
boys wrong numbers, then dash out to the suburbs to eat sushi,
because that's what you do when you're just being young twenty-
somethings.

Best. Life. Ever.

One fine day, a friend and I found ourselves at the casino. She
wanted to have lunch, and I thought, *Why not?* I had just gotten paid, and I had enough spare change, so we grabbed lunch
at one of the cafeteria-style cantinas and sat down, minding
our own business. Soon enough, two older men came over and
started talking. One of the guys approached my friend, and the
other approached me. We didn't mind because they covered our
lunch, and we talked for what seemed like hours. The guy who
was talking to my friend eventually said that he was a business

owner and he helped talent agencies find artists and musicians. *Oh, that's so cool!* I thought.

He told her that he'd like to take her out to dinner and learn more about her. She couldn't believe her luck — a young twenty-two-year-old going out with a business mogul. *Finally,* I thought, *someone who is about business, because she deserves it.* He said he'd have a private car pick her up and take her to the restaurant.

The day came. She sat waiting by the door, me on the other end of the phone wanting to hear the exciting details. She said she was expecting a call that a driver was downstairs, and she'd call me later to tell me all about her date with the guy. Let's just call him Baller Millionaire.

As the evening went on, my friend sat and waited by her front door for hours.

No car.

No driver.

No nothing.

She called me late, feeling let down. I told her to let it go.

Well, the next day he called her and apologized and said he had gotten tied up and asked her if she could come and pick him up from his house. She was on her way.

She called me on her drive. I was a bit confused when she told me the address, because in my mind I didn't know what "baller millionaire" would continue to live on the east side of Detroit (unless they were the illegitimate kind).

"I don't think you should go," I told her. "Turn around and go back home."

"What, girl? Is you crazy? And pass up on this opportunity?"

"What opportunity? He's broke! He's playing you! Any so-called millionaire who supposedly flies back and forth to LA via private jet has zero business on the east side of Detroit at *that address.* I don't think he is who he says he is."

She ignored my advice.

She continued to date the guy, saying he was wining and dining her at amazing restaurants and that he really was a legit millionaire. Baller Millionaire told her they were serving Hamburger Helper on the jet, and when she picked him up from the airport, he had a Tupperware container with leftovers in it.

"Oh-kay," I said as I raised an eyebrow when she told me this story at my house.

Something wasn't right.

A few weeks later, we'd planned to go to Mexico for a girls' trip, and my friend suddenly said she couldn't go.

"Why? Is Baller Millionaire taking you somewhere that week?" I asked. We'd spent months planning this trip, and I was feeling disappointed.

"Well, no, it's not that," she said. She was on the verge of tears as she turned and covered her face with her hands. "I just don't have the money to go."

She collapsed into me, and I held her tight. I couldn't believe what I was hearing.

One bottle of wine later, my friend spilled the tea on Baller Millionaire. He wasn't a baller, and he'd been having her pay for everything with the promise he'd pay her back. She believed him, with his Rolex watch and expensive aftershave; she thought he was just in a hard spot. But after their last date the night before, his phone was disconnected. She cried her soul out to me, and I felt her pain. How could this happen to her? How could she not have seen the signs? He robbed her of her Mexico trip, her self-worth, and her trust in men. She felt not only betrayed but belittled.

It was probably one of the worst experiences of my friend's life because she had been bamboozled by a finesser, and she no longer had the money to go on a vacation to Mexico. Not only did she feel like a fool, but she was also angry.

Remember my friend in chapter 8, the Queen of Schemes, who finessed men all the time? Because it was what she knew, right? Well, Baller Millionaire was doing what he knew: using women to get ahead in life. He didn't have a private plane. He didn't have millions of dollars. And by the way, private jets don't have Tupperware onboard — I know now, I've been on several — and they *damn* for sure don't serve Hamburger Helper for dinner!

But my friend, who saw only the good in folks, had a rude awakening to the reality that not all folks have good intentions.

The good news is, my friend has completely changed her life. I think that experience catapulted her to change. After that she enrolled in college and got her degree in psychology, developed a thriving psychology practice in Chicago, got married to an amazing man, had two adoring children, and became a millionaire in her own right.

Sometimes we have to experience hard lessons to come out stronger. My friend was able to quickly forgive the fake Baller Millionaire, close that chapter in her life, and move on. She didn't dwell on it or pick it apart to analyze it. She accepted it as a lesson and made something amazing out of it instead.

You really can turn lemons into lemonade.

As I said in the previous chapter, when we dwell on what others have done to us, it doesn't do us any good; it only causes ongoing pain. Whether that's chronic physical pain or emotionally draining pain, only we can say when enough is enough and move on from situations. The quickest and easiest way to move past hurt is to forgive our assailants, send them love and light, and turn to the abundance that is waiting for us after we do so.

The Forgiveness Meditation is something that has helped not only me to forgive others and let go but also my clients as well. I encourage you to practice it whenever you need to let go of a situation and move on with your life.

MAGIC ACTION

The Forgiveness Meditation

1. Get in a quiet space and sit in an upright position with your feet firmly planted on the floor. Take an inhalation and exhalation. On the in breath, breathe in love, light, and abundance. On the out breath, breathe out pain, sorrow, and hurt. Repeat this breathing pattern three times.

2. With your eyes closed, imagine the person who caused pain in your life is sitting there in front of you and that you are wiping them away. Pretend you have a cloth in your hand and you're wiping them out of your life. Watch as they disappear from your view. Forgive them for what they've done to you as you wipe them clean from your life. When you complete that action, this person has no ties to you.

3. Now that this person is gone from your life, with your eyes still closed, imagine you are looking at yourself from the outside, and you see a bright white light that goes from the top of your head up, up, and up into the sky, out of the world, and all the way up to Source. Imagine that Source energy is connected to you, sending you love and light and abundance back through the white light and into your body. See the white light filling you up from the top of your head, into your chest, and all the way down to the tips of your toes. Imagine this white light removing any pain, sorrow, or hurt. It is filling you up with love and light.

4. Now, in your mind, see that white light traveling down through the floor and to the center of the earth. Imagine that white light touching the lives of everyone on the planet, healing them, filling them with love and light.

5. Now imagine that white light traveling back to you, sending you love and light and abundance. Sit in this feeling and enjoy this moment.

6. Finally, take a deep breath in and out, open your eyes, and feel the weight of the world fall off your shoulders. You have forgiven the person who has wronged you, and you have let them go. You are filled with love and light and abundance, and you can move on with your day and with your life, spreading love and light wherever you go.

✦ GO EVEN DEEPER ✦

This chapter was deep, and I know that some of you may want to go even deeper to heal your pain. I've created something special to help you to forgive others on a quantum level. Please go to my website to access your Creative Imagining audio: ChloePanta.co/um-5.

Chapter 12

Life Isn't Hard —
People Make It That Way

When we strive to become better than we are,
everything around us becomes better too.

— PAULO COELHO, Brazilian Lyricist, Novelist,
Celebrated Literary Figure

If you haven't read Paulo Coelho's *The Alchemist*, you should. It's about a boy named Santiago who goes on an adventure to find an alchemist in the desert to help him find treasure in the Egyptian pyramids. Along the way he finds love, and, more importantly, he finds himself and his purpose in the world. It's a great book.

The point of the story is that Santiago has to go through hoops and loops to overcome his fears and to come to the realization that no matter what, he has to follow his dreams. Roadblocks will appear, but it is up to us to move them out of the way.

In this chapter, we'll discuss just that: how to overcome roadblocks — and why overcoming them doesn't have to be hard work.

You have heard the phrase "Work hard, play hard" before, yes? Pretty much everybody and their momma has been saying it for years, and to be quite frank, I just don't get it. Why do I want to work hard and play hard? Why can't I just do the work in a leisurely fashion and make my play just as nice? I never understood that saying. Yet a lot of people swear by it — they think that this is the *only* way to get stuff done. I totally beg to differ. I'll tell you why.

Let's go back to chapter 1. Remember when I said that our mind is governed by two parts: the subconscious mind and the conscious mind? The conscious mind is the active, thinking part that makes decisions and focuses on what we're doing right now. The subconscious mind works behind the scenes, storing all our habits and past experiences and silently guiding our actions and feelings.

Just like Oprah said, "You don't become what you want, you become what you believe." If you've gone your entire life watching people bend over backward to accomplish goals or get stuff done, there's a strong probability that you feel you have to do that too to accomplish anything worthwhile in this world.

In order to change our thinking that we have to work extremely hard to find success, we have to go back and re-examine our beliefs. It is our false beliefs that have been instilled in us from an early age that perpetuate the reality a lot of us find ourselves in now. It is intergenerational trauma at its worst.

When we re-examine and question our beliefs, we open our eyes to new possibilities and a world full of abundance, happiness, and tranquility.

My friend Morgan is a great example of what happens when you question your beliefs. After years in a rotten relationship, she had this epiphany that she didn't have to be in a rotten relationship with anyone. She would no longer allow it. She finally understood and believed that she deserved better. Instead of moping around feeling sorry for herself, she brushed her shoulders off and affirmed her new belief that there were better men out there who would add to her happiness. Once she had this new attitude, her entire demeanor changed.

The last time I saw Morgan, she was newly engaged to a doctor who had fallen head over heels in love with her. She had broken the systemic spell of women in her family being in abusive relationships. She'd found her happiness because she changed her beliefs. She stepped fully into her worth. Not only did she believe she was destined for more, she *knew* that she deserved it.

I believe that I deserve to live the life
of my wildest dreams.

When you're faced with an obstacle or a limiting belief, you may be wondering, *Now how the hell am I supposed to overcome that?* Our lives are simply a perception that we choose to believe. It is totally up to us whether we believe that everything will always work out for us no matter what or that life is hard. You'll notice how some folks seem to overcome all odds. Their life is looking lit, and they are on their path to greatness. If you know people like that, realize that they are driven by their perception of how their life is supposed to be. In other words, what they focus on becomes their reality, and they are moving in sync to create the life of their dreams. Then you have other folks whose life feels like it's a constant struggle. They have more bad experiences than good ones, and they will complain to anyone who'll listen. Believe it or not, those folks might be comfortable exactly where they are.

A lot of times we get *rill* comfortable with our lives, and when change is staring us in the face, we don't know what to do. It looks like hard work, that change, and avoiding it keeps us nice and comfy in our current circumstances. My old friend Sonya was the type who never had any money when we wanted to go out. Sonya always complained about how broke she was.

The baby's father was in and out of jail and couldn't be relied on; she didn't even have enough money for diapers for her newborn baby. So a lot of times my friends and I would chip in to help Sonya out. When it was girls' night, we'd cover her tab.

This went on for some time until we all realized that Sonya was never going to help herself get out of her situation. She was broke, but her basic necessities were being covered by either her friends, her family, or the government. She was totally aware of her circumstances, was comfortable being the victim, and had no desire to change. She took zero responsibility for what was going on.

When we stay comfortable, nothing moves forward in our lives, as others progress and seemingly outgrow us. We have to become aware of the areas in our lives where we might have become too comfortable, remove the victim mentality from our way of thinking, and push past fear, barriers, and blocks to create the amazing reality we seek. Sonya could have easily applied for a job and gotten herself out of her situation. With time, she could have moved out of her mother's house and into her own place, raising her child to the best of her ability. Because she was complacent, these options looked like too much responsibility. We don't want to be like Sonya. We are not victims — we are triumphant.

What I focus on becomes my reality.

If you feel like you're ready for a change and you want to throw all those false belief systems in the trash, all you have to do is make a firm affirmation to say "Toodle-oo" to everything that isn't for your highest good and start to design the life you aspire to have. Manifest that life into reality. The moment you decide that the beliefs you hold aren't serving you, you have the power to change your life. There are no rules here. You can manifest what you really want and what you *believe* you can have.

I know this sounds wildly easy peasy, but believe me, it really is. Like I've said before, people make life difficult by buying into the illusion that life is supposed to be difficult. You don't have to live that life anymore. You don't have to wake up in a shitty mood anymore because you have to go to a job you don't like. You no longer have to do mundane everyday things that don't light you up. You are *choosing* to do the things you are doing because they've gotten you this far in life. You have a choice to break through barriers and create the life you really want to live.

Don't take what you have now for granted, though, because what you have right now has allowed you to learn the lessons you needed to learn to level up. Don't just throw away your job because you no longer want to do it. Instead, find something that you want to do that lights you up inside. Find a career that will give you the knowledge to help you grow to become the person you want to be. What can you do that will make you happy and allow you to earn a living? Find that thing and work toward doing that. If waking up on a Monday morning and feeling amazing is important to you, find what it takes to make that your reality. We must move from a place of force and hustle to a place of power, ease, and flow.

If you really want to change your circumstances, you really do have to do the work. All the tools, exercises, and modalities in this book are here to help you manifest the life you're after. But you can't just read this book, put it down, and not implement what you're learning. You have to wholly believe in what you want to achieve and do the work fully. This is the part where most people fail. Don't be one of those people. No half-assin' here, or as my Grumma used to say, stop pussyfootin' around. You're better than that. The life you want is waiting for you to come and grab it by the horns. Go out there and get it!

I create my own reality with the power of my mind.

Remember, you are in control of your life. Overcoming obstacles by just thinking about them isn't going to get you anywhere. When you decide wholly and fully that you are going to do this thing and do it with focus, you will realize that the Universe is on your side, cheering you on, ready to co-create the life you want with you. This starts by letting go of lower thought energetics. Remember? These are thought patterns that create lack or blocks in your subconscious mind and form inner walls against the higher thought energetics of your magic. When you release these negative thoughts, you make way for powerful ones that tell your subconscious mind, *Listen up, fam. We're making changes, OK? It's time to get to work and call in the dreams. Love, money, health, worthiness, and all that stuff, OK?* That's the power of focusing on high vibrational, positive thoughts. We are co-creating with the Universe, and we are walking together through the darkness to get to the light. We are taking a walk with faith to create a fruitful life.

Choosing faith over fear = a fruitful life

In the following Magic Action, I'm going to take you on a journey to swap those negative vibes with up-leveling ones. If you put in the work and practice these steps, you'll be well on your way to creating a life of pure bliss, ease, and flow.

MAGIC ACTION

Unlocking Your Limiting Beliefs

1. *Understand what your limiting beliefs are.* Sometimes these are things we've learned from our childhood; sometimes they're things we've acquired as adults, from conversations with friends; and some are things we've

picked up along the way that we thought were cool. Remember, you are the creator of your life. You're the star of the show, the director, the makeup artist, the producer, the everything. Once you become aware of your limiting beliefs, you can cut them out and create new beliefs in their place.

2. *Release those limiting beliefs from your subconscious mind.* Do you find yourself saying or thinking things like this?

- *I'm not good at dating. All the good folks are taken.*
- *I wish I had money so I could do more with my life, but I'm stuck.*
- *Maybe one day I'll buy a house...when I get around to saving money.*
- *I should be better at my job.*
- *I should lose weight.*

These are expressions of your limiting beliefs. Change them to positive beliefs by changing the words you use. When you have a clear understanding of your actions, that's when they manifest into your actual world. Remove these phrases from your vocabulary:

- *I can't...*
- *I never...*
- *I should...*
- *I'll try...*
- *Maybe one day...*
- *I wish...*
- *I'm not good at...*

3. *Swap out the negative beliefs with positive ones.* When we drop negative phrases from our vocabulary, we're up-leveling our lives. We're ditching those self-limiting

thoughts from our subconscious mind and charging ahead to craft the life we've been envisioning. To do that, replace every negative thought with a positive one. Instead of negative phrases, use words like:

- *I can...*
- *I can now...*
- *I choose to...*
- *I will...*
- *I am...*
- *Starting today...*
- *I'm improving in...*
- *I'm doing...*

Make sure that you are crystal clear on what your new positive phrases are. Instead of saying, *Maybe one day I'll buy a house*, replace it with *I will buy a house in the next six months*. And work toward that specific goal, making it your living reality. Take ownership of your life and really mean what you say.

4. *Know that your goals might change, and that's OK.* As we grow, our needs change, our goals change. Be OK with that and be OK with re-evaluating your goals and needs as time goes on. Instead of buying a house in the city, now you have a need for more peace and quiet, so you've decided to buy a house in the country. Be OK with change as you grow.

Chapter 13

Take Your Power Back

*When I dare to be powerful, to use my strength
in the service of my vision, then it becomes less and less
important whether I am afraid.*

— AUDRE LORDE, American Writer, Philosopher,
Civil Rights Activist

In 2009, I had an awakening experience with someone I no longer communicate with. I had just moved to Northville, a small town outside of Detroit. For those who don't know, Northville is an affluent town where all the homes are beautifully designed, sitting on acres and acres of land. My mom's boyfriend at the time, Roc, co-signed on my lease because my credit was too bad for me to get something in my own name. I moved in with my bedroom set and furniture I thrifted from secondhand stores with my mom and Grumma, and I was elated. Finally, a place of my own in the town of my dreams.

I had a dream of starting an online business selling hair products. My initial idea was to ask one of my closest friends to go into business with me. But when I shared my dream with her, she was being extra AF.

"Who would buy anything from you?" she said, picking at her old manicured nails.

It's time for a fill-in, I thought. "What do you mean?" I asked, perplexed. I guess I didn't expect this type of reaction from her. "You mean, you don't think I can do it?"

"A lot of businesses fail. Why would yours be any different? I don't think you should start a business. You'd have too much competition. It's too risky, and you don't have the money to do it anyway."

I thought about that for some time. I was angry that she had the audacity to say that to me and also hurt because she didn't believe in me. At this time in my life, I wasn't thinking about the expansiveness that is the Universe. The Universe is so expansive, there is more than enough for every single human being on this planet to be successful and live in abundance. As I've said throughout this book, when we carry a lack mentality, we only create more lack in our lives. And because I was afraid to step into my power and truly become my best self, I allowed someone else's beliefs to become my own, and doubt crept into my mind that wasn't there before. *What if she's right?* I thought.

Later on, I realized this was someone I was going to have to cut out of my life — for good. I decided to start my online business on my own. It was a big risk because I invested all my savings in this business, and if it failed, I would be out of my savings. On the other hand, I was employed. I could always make it back and start again. That's what prompted me to make the move. And I was successful. I was able to do something I loved and earn additional income alongside what I got at my job. I obviously proved my friend wrong, but I also did something that was completely scary to me at the time by taking a chance on faith.

When we embody our magic and fully step into our power, we are allowing shifts to take place in our paradigms and programs. When this happens, we are removing patterns that were previously keeping us stuck and replacing them with thought patterns that are creating lasting change.

Know and understand that your journey and your path are not meant for everyone to comprehend. There will be times when others will test you with questions, doubts, and uncertainties. If that happens, see it as merely your own subconscious fears coming to the surface. Your subconscious mind is saying to you, *Are you sure you wanna do this? Are you really ready to go all in?* When someone tells you you aren't good enough at something, for example, ask yourself, *Is this a limiting belief that I myself carry deep down inside? Or is this a belief that doesn't belong to me?* When we do something that is outside of the beliefs or comfort zones of those closest to us, it can be scary for them (because you have the guts to pursue it) but also scary for us (because we are being vulnerable and opening up to them, sharing with them our passions and our beliefs).

When I shared with my friend my thoughts on opening an online business, I thought she'd be happy for me. But because of her own limiting beliefs and insecurities, she reacted with feelings of envy toward me and fear — fear that if I were to succeed, I'd leave her behind. What she didn't know was that I wanted to take her with me and share in the success that was to come.

When we experience envy, we are seeing something in someone else that we want for ourselves. We have a fear or a limiting belief that we can't achieve what that person is achieving. But what envy can teach us is that what that person has is actually an exact mirror of what is possible for each of us.

I remember when I used to be envious of all the girls who had tiny waists and outrageous curves. I'd see them on all the music videos — video vixens. I'd get so envious that I had to stop watching music videos altogether because it affected my self-esteem. Little did I know that what they were reflecting to me was something I myself could achieve. My envy was a sign that I had to heal those areas in my life and that I needed to do inner work on loving myself more. Later in life, this envy prompted me to become a vegetarian and to take care of myself. It prompted me to fall in love with running, going to the gym, taking walks, being in nature, and just moving my body in some form every single day.

My body is strong, perfect, whole, and complete.

With time, I not only let go of my envious feelings toward all the beautiful video vixens, but I embraced my own beauty and became extremely comfortable and confident with my body, loving it and taking extra care of it. Now it is something I adore, and I feel as confident and beautiful as the video vixens I once envied.

The Law of Divine Oneness

Whether you believe it or not, you and your nosy neighbor who always stares out the window at you are derived from a single source of oneness, a single collective of universal consciousness. In other words, we as human beings are all connected to one another.

Depending on what you believe in, you may feel that we come from one Source or one Light or Love or that we are the source of Infinite Intelligence. We all came here to earth to experience the expressive uniqueness each one of us has. We came here to experience emotions that are the opposite of love (fear, hate, scarcity, anger, envy, jealousy, etc.) in order to find our path back to love. Our path back to our authentic, true selves. Back to oneness and wholeness, and back to one another.

When we attack others or react to them in a negative way, it in turn hurts us, because we are all divinely connected. And because we are connected, retaliating against someone is only retaliating against a part of ourselves. We must do the work to heal our wounds, love ourselves fully, and embrace ourselves for who we are. The Universe is always supporting expansion, love, and creativity. We are here in this world to experience life as creative beings. When we lean into our expansiveness, the Universe works with us, supports us, and cheers us on to manifest our aspirations and dreams. When we co-create with the Universe, our lives are filled with ease and flow, because we're not forcing or resisting. When we go with the natural flow of life and co-create in an easy, calm manner, we attract what it is we want. Thinking back on all the most important things I've manifested in my life — my husband, my house, my business — I see that I have manifested all of them with such ease. When we try to force something to happen, it isn't coming to us in a natural state of flow, and we encounter resistance.

My friend Neha had a dream to open a restaurant in downtown Detroit. She started a blog that became wildly successful, and she decided it was time to take her dream to the next level. She is an amazing cook who always made me and my friends fantastic meals, throwing dinner parties whenever she could. But her husband, despite her success in the kitchen, didn't want her to do it. She told me one day that she felt torn. Deep down she knew that this was her passion and she really wanted to pursue her dream, but her husband wasn't supportive and would knock down any idea she shared with him.

I could see that her husband was in fact mirroring doubts that she herself was having. Could she be successful as a restaurateur? Where would she get the money from? Could she qualify for a loan? They were also trying to start a family. How would she run a restaurant and raise their child at the same time? So many questions ran through her mind that she was wearing herself out. I advised Neha to answer each question for herself and to make a list of which ones seemed easy and which ones felt challenging.

She eventually found out about programs for small businesses to qualify for loans, and she was able to get pre-approved for the loan amount she needed for her restaurant. She also knew that starting a family at the same time as opening a restaurant would be challenging. After discussing it with her husband, they decided to hold off on having children until the business was in a stable place, with staff and a manager to oversee the operations when she couldn't be there. She realized that her husband only wanted to validate her obstacles and challenge her to overcome them so she would be prepared for what was to come. She just needed to face her fears head-on.

If you're experiencing something similar, where a loved one is challenging your dreams, you have to dig down deep inside and determine what is really happening. Are these your own limiting beliefs wanting validation that you can overcome them and that you're ready to tackle them head-on? Or are they *not* your limiting beliefs, but your loved one's own lack mentality staring you in the face?

Now, you may be asking, *How will I know which it is?* I got you. You'll know if they are the other person's limiting beliefs if you don't feel a pang of insecurity or other emotion deep down inside when they come up. For instance, someone can tell you, "You'll never amount to anything." If that statement doesn't hold weight to you, you'll know it is that person's limiting belief, not yours — it has zero to do with you. But if they tell you you'll never amount to anything and it *does* trigger a reaction or emotion within you, you know you've got some inner work to do. You need to resolve that limiting belief inside you so you can attract more abundance in your life and reach new heights.

Unfortunately, there are people in this world who do thrive

on hurting others and instilling false beliefs in them. You take your power back and protect it from these types of people by not allowing them to get a triggering response from you and by removing yourself from their presence if necessary to keep yourself safe. It is up to you to protect your power by knowing your own limiting beliefs and working through them. When you remove those blocks within, folks with lower thought energetics lose their ability to trigger you.

Does all that sound complicated? I promise you, it really isn't. I'm going to share with you a two-part Magic Action process not only for cleansing yourself of limiting beliefs — those from your own mind and those imposed by others — but also for replacing those beliefs with a whole new way of thinking. If you feel that you have given your power away to others by allowing them to impose their limiting beliefs on you, these potent exercises will help you to take your power back, once and for all. When doing these exercises, choose one limiting belief to unpack at a time, and work through it fully before moving to the next limiting belief that you want to tackle.

MAGIC ACTION

Part 1: Identifying Your Limiting Beliefs

In this exercise, we will work on identifying your limiting beliefs. Know that this process takes time and may not always stick on the first try. But with daily practice, you can push past your mental barriers and thrive, letting in abundance and manifesting your dreams and goals.

1. Get in a quiet place and reflect on your limiting beliefs. Identify where they came from. They could be from your

childhood, your adolescence, or even your adult life, picked up from family or friends. Journal about your thoughts.

2. Pick one limiting belief you'd like to work on. Now, in your journal, explore your limiting belief more deeply by responding to the following prompts:

- What trigger, emotion, or block do you want to move through? What's keeping you feeling stuck or uncertain in a particular situation?
- What situation or person is triggering your limiting belief?
- What emotions are you feeling around this person or situation?
- Describe the emotion you are feeling. Is it a sensation in your body? Where are you feeling it?
- Why is this emotion being triggered? What sense of lack or limiting belief needs to be addressed?
- If you had to give your emotional sensation an age, what age would it be? (Is this a familiar sensation you felt during your childhood or from an event that triggered you as a young adult?)
- What are you sensing you need from this emotion? (Is it safety, security, worthiness, love, affection, etc.?)
- When in your life have you felt this need most acutely? (Childhood, adolescence, early adulthood, etc.?)
- Can you go back to a very specific memory of a time when this emotion was triggered?
- Why do you still lack in this area of your life? What can you do to give yourself what you need in order to release this limiting belief?

MAGIC ACTION

Part 2: Reinforcing a New Way of Thinking

Once you've completed part 1 of the exercise, the actionable items listed below will help you to dig down deep and find the root cause of your limiting belief. Then, you'll create a new belief that supports you manifesting what it is that you want in your life. Let's say your limiting belief was in *a lack of money*. Maybe a lack mentality was instilled in you in your childhood because your family never had enough and you were repeatedly told no when you asked for basic necessities or things you wanted. Now, as an adult, this lack mentality shows up as you feeling the need to hold on to your money and not to spend on things you need or want, because you're afraid there may not be enough left for a rainy day. Once you drill down and identify that root cause of your limiting belief, you can replace it with a new belief in *an abundance of money*.

1. ***Get to the root.*** Reflecting on the journaling you did in the previous Magic Action, go back to your childhood to identify what is repeating itself over and over again in your life. This is the root cause of what's triggering your limiting belief, whether it is a lack of security, shortness of money, feelings of unworthiness, lack of safety, or a fear of something.

2. ***Decide if it's true.*** Again, go back to your childhood and ask yourself if this limiting belief is the truth. What about this limiting belief do you feel is true to you in your world today?

3. ***Face the fear.*** What are you afraid of? What is it about this limiting belief that is keeping you playing small? Why are you afraid of this limiting belief? Write out the worst-that-could-happen scenario around this limiting

belief and develop a plan to overcome it if it were to happen. For instance, if you are afraid to leave your job and start a new career for lack of stability, the worst that could happen is that you could lose your job and it takes longer than expected to find a new one in your new chosen career path. Maybe it will take six months instead of three months to find a new job because you haven't learned all the skills needed for the new job. If you are fearful of losing your stability, think of ways to diversify your income to create more stability, such as by saving money from every paycheck, picking up a part-time job, or investing. There are plenty of ways to create stability to feel safe and secure and release the lack mentality. Work through your fears and worst-that-could-happens to find the solution to your limiting belief.

4. *Create new beliefs and reinforce them in your everyday life.* When you release an old limiting belief, you now have room to create a new belief system. Instead of thinking in lack, think of how abundant you are and how the Universe will always provide for you. If insecurity creeps in, remind yourself, *I am secure, I am safe, I am protected,* to consciously rewrite the old thought patterns. But remember, if you don't feel it or believe it, it won't happen for you. Always envision your new belief, feel it, and take action to make it your new reality.

When doing this exercise, the emotions that come up can be powerful. If you feel that you need extra support, be sure to consult with a therapist or life coach for help working through these challenging areas of your life.

Chapter 14

Re-creating Your Reality

*I'm going to do what I want to do. I'm going to be
who I really am. I'm going to figure out what that is.*

— EMMA WATSON, British Actress, Women's Rights Activist,
UN Women's Goodwill Ambassador

In 2012, I was quietly engrossed in my work, just like on any other day in the workplace, when an email notification disrupted the humdrum of the office. What made it different was that this email had everyone's attention – the entire company was copied on it.

The subject line sent a jolt of dread coursing through me: "If you own a gray Ford Explorer, your car is being towed..."

As those words flashed on my screen, time seemed to slow down. I could feel the blood draining from my face. Panic set in as I peered over the edge of my cubicle, my heart pounding in my chest. There, right before my disbelieving eyes, was my beloved gray Ford Explorer being towed away from the company parking lot. The worst part? All my co-workers were watching, their curiosity piqued by the unfolding spectacle.

Without a moment's hesitation, I sprinted toward the exit, my mind racing as I tried to make sense of this surreal nightmare. Outside, I confronted the tow truck driver, desperation in my voice as I demanded an explanation for this sudden and humiliating ordeal.

"Your car's being repossessed, miss," the towman said, his tone indifferent to the turmoil erupting within me. "I guess you haven't been making the payments on it."

My world came crashing down with those words. It wasn't me who hadn't been making the payments.

Remember the red Grand Am my dad got me for my birthday? That car was stolen. He got me another one — and that one was repossessed. He said he would get me a new car in a couple of weeks.

Lo and behold, he did. And he promised me that he would pay the car note, even when I offered to pay. "Naw, Chloe, I got it, I'll take care of it for you."

"OK, Daddy." My relief at being spared a car payment mingled with a lingering sense of unease. I had a gut feeling that something just wasn't right.

After a few months of his not paying that car note, they finally figured out where the car was and came to collect it. Outside my place of work.

Deep down inside I knew this day would come — because it had happened before, and I had to ask myself: *Why would this time be different?*

Because of my embarrassment at work, my manager allowed me to take the rest of the day off. I called a cab to take me home and cried my eyes out on my living room floor. I felt like my life was spiraling out of control. What was happening to me? I had no car, I had no support system, and I had no idea what I was going to do to get my life in order. I hated my job. My manager sexually harassed me all the time, and my director — a woman who was his manager — *didn't do a damn thing about it.* I felt trapped. I just felt like *giving the fuck up* because I couldn't see any way out of this situation.

After I spent who knows how long curled in a ball on the floor, I made a decision that I would not give up and that I would change my life for the better. I didn't know how, but it was going to happen, no matter what. I called around to dealerships, and a Chevy dealer told me to come on down, they had a special program for people like me who were rebuilding their credit. Even though I was unsure if it would work for me, a couple of hours later, I drove off the lot in a brand-new Chevy Malibu, which ended up being my most loved car. I drove to my mom's house to show it off, elated that I finally had something *in my name* — with no co-signer and no empty promises that would only break my heart. I told myself that from that day forward I would never let me down and I would always come through for myself — and I always have.

Being poor was something I struggled with as a young adult. I didn't have parents who had generational wealth or trust funds, who went to prestigious universities and knew all the right people who I could learn from. Our family wasn't surrounded by wealth or people who I could rub elbows with and whose knowledge I could soak up. It's been hard to admit it, and even saying it today is a struggle: I was poor. I refused to admit it to myself back then, even though my finances were a mess. I had zero financial knowledge and felt the topic was too complicated to even begin to comprehend. I had zero knowledge of how to manage my money, and that was why I lived paycheck to paycheck. I had shiny object syndrome — buying things I had no business buying before paying my bills.

It wasn't until I started a corporate job out of state that I truly began to understand the importance of money management and excellent credit. One day, I watched my co-worker Samantha negotiate her brand-new car payment over the phone with a car dealership. Where I came from, you took what you got approved for, even if it wasn't what you wanted. You got what your credit could afford you. But my co-worker was the epitome of what I wanted to become — someone who had their shit together so I would no longer need to depend on anyone ever again for anything.

And then it began.

Samantha and I became close friends, and her close friends also became my friends. They weren't all from money, but their stories were different from the ones I'd always heard from my old friends. Instead of complaining about needing to put gas in their car to get to work or spending their last ten dollars on a bag of weed or what bum didn't call them after the club last night, they complained about not becoming bridesmaids at some other girl's wedding or about trying to conceive through IVF. It was a completely different ball game. I decided to learn everything I could from Samantha. "Pay your bills on time, even if it's just the minimum balance. Spend below your means. Only use your credit card knowing you can pay off the entire balance before the end of the month. Set a budget..." She taught me so much financial sense that I got my first credit card in my name through her help.

As I spent less and less time with my old friends and more and more time with my new friends, my life was changing right before my eyes. I became more aware of my spending habits. I stopped buying new clothes and shoes every week. I started to do my own hair again so I wouldn't have to spend so much money at the salon. Instead of getting fake nails, I did my natural nails myself.

As time went on, I got in the habit of saving money for a rainy day. I knew I wanted to do something with my life, but with so many possibilities, I couldn't choose just one. I decided that when the time was right, I'd use my savings to start a business of some sort and live out my dreams, traveling the world full-time or writing full-time. Something would come through — I knew it would — I just didn't know what or how at the time. I kept working in my job, enjoying my newly built friendships, and working on myself mentally, physically, and emotionally.

When we want something but we aren't sure how to get it, we have to expand ourselves to other possibilities, people, and opportunities. I had no idea about finance, but I wanted to improve my situation. The universe guided me to the right people to help me to help myself. When we ask, we shall receive. It may be in a way you hadn't imagined, but if you are open to new possibilities, the Universe will guide you to finding the answers you seek.

The Universe will bring you what you need
if only you let go and trust the process.

How to Become Expansive

Becoming expansive means we believe that something is possible for us to have. (In my case, it was financial sense and rebuilding my credit.) When we see others who have what we want, expanding ourselves shows our subconscious mind that that life is possible for us too. When we are expanded, our subconscious mind pushes out all the stuff that no longer serves us and creates space to bring forth all of what we want. That's why it's so important to work through issues that happened when we were younger. All those false belief systems must be released from our subconscious mind to make way for new and expanded ways of thinking. Your brand-new house. Your new Tesla. Your brand-new, big, 'bout it bank account. All these things require *expansiveness*.

When we have limiting beliefs or feel stuck living with a scarcity mindset, we are telling the Universe and our subconscious mind, *No, I don't want that stuff. I'm cool being broke.*

Yep, keep sending me bills in the mail I'm never gonna pay. Yep, keep allowing me to attract broke, busted folks. Yep, yep, yep! The Universe and your subconscious mind will in turn say, *OK, cool. Imma keep you broke then.* The thing with the Universe and your subconscious mind is that they don't know what good or bad is, what's right or wrong. They simply bring forth to you what you already believe in, deep down inside. Whatever truly lies at your core is what you're gonna get in return. Like I've said before, you can keep telling yourself, *I want a million dollars,* but if deep down inside *you know* that's not possible for you, then hey, the Universe and the subconscious are gonna feel the same way about it. You can't keep lying to yourself or the Universe. It's smarter than that. And so are you. You have to *believe* with a *firm affirmation* that the million-dollar bank balance is a sure thing for you. And if you don't, try for something a bit less that feels comfortable to you. As you feel more comfortable with a lesser number, expand yourself to allow that abundance to flow into your life.

You become expanded once you release blocks from your life that are keeping you small. These blocks can be core beliefs that have been instilled in you since childhood and have created the life you live today. If you grew up broke, have broken relationships, are currently broke, and feel trapped, it means you have work to do before you can become unbroke. Understand? You can't have a broke person's belief system and think you're gonna call in expansiveness. It just doesn't work like that. You have to remove those old, crusty wounds and make room for new and expansive beliefs. You have to get to your core and step into your whole Authentic Self.

In truth, we are already whole, but we lost our awareness of it along our way. The universe is simply trying to bring it back to our awareness so that we will return to that wholeness and live the most authentic life that we were meant to live. It requires us to peel back the layers that we've built up around ourselves living in this world. Those layers are the shame, the guilt, the unworthiness, the lack mentality, the scarcity mindset, feeling invisible, the feelings of doubt and of being unloved. When we do, we discover that we are all magical, powerful beings and that the key to creating the life we love lies deep within us. Our untapped magic is waiting at the core of our being to be released, to allow abundance into our lives.

To me, living your most authentic life means living in a state of joy, feeling safe and secure, having fulfillment, and being guided by purpose. It means waking up every day excited about your life and all the possibilities that lie ahead. It means being true to yourself and living a life that aligns with your values and passions.

But, you might be asking, *how do I get there? How do I go from feeling stuck and unhappy to living out my dreams?* As I've mentioned throughout this book, in order to change your life, you first must change the way you think, unblocking core wounds in your life and changing your beliefs and actions. Once you believe that the life you want is possible for you to have, you come closer to living it. When you follow up your change of belief with releasing any old limiting beliefs and follow through with aligned Magic Action, you will get there. But if you continue to stay stuck and live with a scarcity mindset, you'll keep replaying the same old life over and over again.

Anything is possible for you if only you believe.

When you believe that what you want is really possible for you to have and that you are worthy of living a fulfilled life, you then must identify what it is that you want. I've said this many times throughout this book because I want this message to be so ingrained in your mind that it's impossible for you to forget. I know identifying what you want can sometimes be tricky, especially with many of us being stuck in a state of shoulda, woulda, coulda, thinking that it's too late for us. But it is never too late. We've been conditioned to believe that pursuing our dreams is some impossible feat, mainly because those who conditioned us either have been too afraid to chase after their own dreams or have failed to find success in them. And I totally get it. We are the products of our environment — but that doesn't have to be the end of our story.

Most of the clients who come to work with me struggle with taking action. They procrastinate because their goal looks like an eight-hundred-pound gorilla that they don't know how to handle. So they talk about what they want to do and dream about it all day, but they don't do anything to make it a reality. When we break down our big, bad goals into smaller, actionable steps that are aligned with our authentic selves, we become consistent. Like me when I tricked myself into going to the gym every day. I told myself going to the gym was like brushing my teeth — it just had to be done. There were no ifs, ands, or buts about it. And that's what I did. I set my alarm to go off between five and five thirty in the morning, and I'd be up and at it every day to get time in at the gym. And this is now my life. I love going to the gym because I love how it feels to take such good care of myself and my body. I am so in love with myself that it only makes sense to take excellent care of my body. I am stronger. I am happier. I am healthier. I am leaner. All because of a simple little trick of convincing myself that going to the gym was like brushing my teeth.

If we want something bad enough, we're going to do what it takes to make it happen. Even on days we don't feel like it, we push through our resistance and we up-level our lives by getting it done. That's called growth, that's called persistence, that's called consistency. That's called mastery.

That's called magic.

When we truly are the masters of our lives, we transform by quantum leaps and bounds, ready to overcome anything that comes our way.

We *Homo sapiens* are not here because of mere luck. We've outlived eight other species of human beings because we are *strong*. When it comes to getting what you want in this life, you must be strong. Strong in your mind, body, spirit, and soul. When everything is aligned internally, that is when everything begins to fall in place in your outside world and you begin to live the life of your dreams.

I can't stress this enough: you will need to get comfortable being uncomfortable. When you begin to grow, you begin to up-level. Up-leveling requires doing things that you haven't done before. That may mean speaking in front of a large group of people to be the next in line for director at your organization. Being uncomfortable may mean changing your eating habits to become healthier and to overcome any disease you may be facing. It may mean dumping your partner because they're holding you back. It may mean downsizing your home so you can reduce your expenses and become cash rich and live below your means. It may mean going back to school after forty. It may mean moving across the country for a new, unexpected opportunity. It may mean coming out to your family. It may mean going against your old beliefs because they've changed. Whatever it is, you need to face your fears head-on and let them know who's the boss. Because at the end of the day, you run the show. You get to decide how the movie's going to end. You get to decide that it's time for a change. When you take action and you're willing to step out on faith, that's when your life will never be the same again.

Another important thing to do when you're changing your life is to surround yourself with people who are ready to cheer you on and support you in your goals and your journey. Lots of folks say, "You are the average of the five folks you spend the most time with." Take a look at those folks. Are they people who you want to be like? Are they uplifting you, encouraging you, and working on their own goals and dreams? Folks who play small will stay small and will only make excuses, complain, and stay stuck in their current lives for years to come. If you're constantly hanging around folks who are broke and poor and are cool with being broke and poor and stuck, well... you might need to take a look in the mirror. When you surround yourself with people who are on your team and who are inspiring and successful, it only fuels your fire to help you achieve your own dreams. There are plenty of people out there who are ready to support and encourage you to go after the life you want — and if they don't, bench their ass and move on to the next.

It's crucial to remember that when you're creating your reality, it isn't just about changing on the behavioral level, but about changing internally too. That's where the real magic happens. The exercise below will help you do just that.

MAGIC ACTION

Creating Transformational Change from the Inside Out

1. *Identify your goals.* Take time to identify what it is you really want in this life. This could be professional growth, financial stability, starting a new business or hobby, having an amazing relationship, etc. Get clear on this goal.

2. *Create a plan.* Once you know what it is that you want, create a plan. Write down what you want and your plan to achieve it. Break down your steps into bite-size actionable items that you can accomplish easily and effortlessly and check off your list.

3. *Go back to your childhood.* Return to chapter 13 to complete Magic Action, part 1, "Identifying Your Limiting

Beliefs." Repeat this step until you feel the weight fall off your shoulders and know that you can carry on to the next step in this Magic Action.

4. *Develop self-awareness.* As you transform through your life, you'll notice you will start to feel different, act different, and become different. Spend time on your personal growth by reflecting on your thoughts, actions, and behaviors. Identify and write down any patterns that may be holding you back.

5. *Challenge your way of thinking.* Limiting beliefs can keep us stuck. If we're trying to break through barriers, we have to remove feelings of scarcity. Replace your lower thought energetics with higher thought energetics that uplift and empower you.

6. *Overcome roadblocks along the way.* There will be tests. You will face obstacles. It's the Universe's way of making sure we're prepared for what's coming and that it's really what we want. If you feel there's a block that's keeping you from getting what you want, persevere and overcome it. It could come in the form of a lower-paying job that might be blocking the higher-paying job we're calling in. It could be a partner who has some of the qualities we seek, but not all of them. Overcome these roadblocks by standing firm in your beliefs and by focusing on what you truly want and knowing that you deserve it and that it is coming. If you pass the test by saying no to the lesser thing, you become receptive to even greater abundance.

7. *Surround yourself with amazing folks.* These can be people you aspire to be like, folks you look up to, or friends and family who support you and encourage you along your journey. These are the people who can uplift you when you're feeling stuck, who can cheer you on to keep going and not give up on your dreams.

8.   *Take aligned action steps.* When you're operating from your Authentic Self, taking consistent steps, no matter how small, toward your goals equals transformation. This puts you in alignment with where you want to go in life.

9.   *Celebrate your wins.* Celebrate each win along the way, whether big or small. If it's moving to the second round of interviews for your dream job, congratulate yourself. If it's getting pre-qualified for your new home loan, be excited about the progress you've made. If it's booking your one-way flight across the country to live your dream life in your dream city, be proud of yourself for taking that huge leap forward. This will keep you motivated and allow you to continue to take aligned action toward achieving your goals.

PART 4

Change Your
MIND
to Change Your
REALITY

Chapter 15

Using Your Magic for the Greater Good

You can't force the outside world to change.
You must first change the inside.

— CHLOE PANTA, Writer of Books, Coacher of Folks,
Native Detroiter

When you realize your significance to this world, it not only affects you, but it affects the *world*. It brightens someone's day when you smile at them. It gives a hopeless person hope when you recognize them as you pass by. It sends out so much love and light when you buy an unsheltered person a meal or a cup of coffee. The small things you do add up, creating positive change in our planet. You are needed, and you are loved. Always remember that. Your very existence is creating a positive ripple effect on this earth.

Never stop being your kind, generous self. Even if you think no one is noticing, there is always someone who will be affected by your kindness and generosity. Your infectious smile; your obnoxious laugh. *You matter.* Always remember that. Now and forever.

When I was seventeen, I wanted to be a fashion designer. I wanted to go to New York or Paris to study at Parsons School of Design. My dream was to become the next great designer. I took up fashion designing in high school, and I loved creating designs I could imagine myself wearing or some celebrity strutting the red carpet in.

One day my mom asked me what college I wanted to go to, and I told her I wanted to go to design school.

"Design school? You mean for architecture?" she said while she sat at the dining room table folding clothes.

"No, Mommi, I'm talking about fashion design."

"Is that even a real degree? What can you do with that?"

"I can learn how to design clothes..." I could tell by the way her eyebrows furrowed that this was a losing battle. My confidence dwindled as I questioned my own beliefs. *Would I be successful? Who would want to buy clothes from me or wear them on the runway?*

She later told me that those types of degrees don't pay the bills if you don't make it. I felt hurt because to me it meant she didn't believe that I could succeed. With this new fear of failure planted in me, I settled for something else.

But my dream was only deferred, not dead and gone. Though I didn't get a degree in fashion design, it didn't stop me from learning. When I moved to my loft in downtown Detroit, I had the incredible opportunity to meet many other creative individuals. Fashion designers. Hat designers. Shoe designers. People who transformed literal trash into beautiful art. I felt I had my Parsons right in my very own backyard. And through these creatives, I got introduced to some very important people who wanted to put on a fashion show for a neighborhood in our downtown. They put me in charge of everything, and it was a dream come true. I got to work curating designs for models I handpicked, setting up music and the theme of the show. I got to put on my very own fashion show where my curated designs were front and center for all of Detroit to see! It was wild, magical, and so much fun. My designs may not have graced the runway at New York Fashion Week, but this was mine, and I created it. Despite my mother's cautious words, which were only meant to protect me, I was able to still live out my dream.

Even if it seems far away from your reality,
what you want is coming to you.

I tell this story to show you that even when you think your dream is deferred, it can become yours. It doesn't have to "dry up / like a raisin in the sun," as the great poet Langston Hughes once wrote. You can change your world by focusing on what you want and bring your manifestations to you with full force. You have the power to create something that feels so out of reach for you and make it your own. When I was seventeen, the world was my oyster. But as time went on, I saw that sometimes, a lot of times, things just don't go as planned. Dreams become deferred as the demands of life take center stage. Bills pile up and money is scarce, and the need to survive in a world you have to figure out on your own becomes the priority. But once I got tired of living in a place of scarcity and fear, I thought I'd try the opposite. What was the worst that could happen? I'd already hit rock bottom before, and I knew what that felt like, but I also knew it wasn't *forever*. I'd get back up again and try again and again and again until I made it.

The one thing we can learn about our magic is that is doesn't go away. We each have our own special magic deep down inside us that can never be taken away. Once we use it not only as a source of good but to change our way of thinking for the better, we start moving in the direction of the thing that we want the most. Little synchronicities add up, and we are catapulted toward the world we never knew was possible for us, until it's right in front of us.

Back in 2006, before the devastating market crash in 2008, I was twenty, and I was considering a career as a loan officer but then changed my mind. I decided to become a real estate agent instead. It was the time to be a loan officer, too, because the way loans were being handed out, you could drive into work one day in a Pontiac and the next week you could be driving off the lot in a big, 'bout it Benz. This happened to my friend Dwayne, who I met at the loan officer training institute. I was studying at the adjoining building taking a real estate course to become a licensed real estate agent. I wanted to drive a big, 'bout it Benz, too.

Some months later, Dwayne and I met up for lunch to catch up after our classes ended. "Me and the boys are going to Miami next week. You should come," Dwayne said. We were having lunch together, and he couldn't help himself — he was elated to show me his new Benz parked right outside.

"When did this happen?" I asked, pointing from him to his new ride and seeing his smile widen.

"You know that thing I was telling you about? The loan officer shit, right?"

"Yeah?"

"Well, I'm doing really well, Clo. We have this special program we put folks in so they can buy a house, even if they have bad credit." He looked around to see if anybody was in earshot and then whispered to me, "Even if they can't really afford the house…it's insane, baby girl. You don't know how easy this money is." He sat up straight again and said in his normal voice, "Things are going amazing!" He beamed from ear to ear as we toasted to his success. "You should still do it. It's not too late."

I thought about this for a moment: Clo in a big, 'bout it Benz. *No more relying on my dad to pay my car note. I'd be stuntin' on Belle Isle, and I'd be the baddest they'd ever seen…. But I don't know, yo….If people can't afford the houses they're buying, then that's not a good thing. Think Imma steer clear of this one….*

"Nah, I'm straight," I said. "I'm still new to the real estate industry, and riding this temporary wave is going to have consequences. I don't want to have any part in it, but I'm happy for you. I'm working on another project anyway."

Little did I know that the housing market would crash in less than two years and Dwayne would be out of a job and out of his big, 'bout it Benz. I recall the last time we spoke he was working at the Chili's where we had gone for lunch.

Now, I'm not saying Dwayne was a bad person, but when we do things that aren't for the greater good, these things have consequences. The point I am trying to home in on is that we shouldn't profit off others in a way that will negatively impact humanity. It took the housing market a year and a half to begin to bounce back. But it took much longer for so many folks to get back on their feet. *Much longer.* And some folks never recovered. The US was in a recession, folks lost their jobs, and many of my friends and acquaintances fell victim to such schemes. It wasn't a good time for a lot of people, and living in the Midwest, we felt it pretty hard.

This is an example of how things can go badly if we try to get over on people. But here's how things can go incredibly great for us when we help others, even in unassuming ways.

Fast-forward to when I moved to California and took on consulting.

In the bustling skies above San Francisco, I embarked on a routine flight back home to LA. My work in consulting often meant shuttling between cities, but this particular journey had an unexpected twist.

As I settled into my seat, I noticed the gentleman next to me, a fellow traveler. There's a unique unspoken connection between people who share the same heritage, especially when they find themselves in unfamiliar surroundings. It's a nod of acknowledgment, a silent affirmation that says, "I see you."

We did the nod to each other.

Our flight took off, and we each settled in with our bags in front of our feet. The man beside me, Anthony, finally removed his headphones and with a polite gesture asked if he could place his backpack in the empty seat between us. I had been eyeing it too. We both sought some extra legroom, courtesy of the middle seat vacancy. He placed his backpack in the chair, and I pulled my Neverfull bag (which always seems to be overflowing) next to his backpack.

"Where are you headed?" Anthony inquired, breaking the ice.

"LA," I replied, offering him an Altoid. "And you?"

"I have a layover in LA, then it's back home to Chicago."

"That's incredible! I'm originally from Detroit," I responded, perhaps a bit too enthusiastically.

"Really? That's cool. How long have you been in LA?"

"Almost six months now."

Anthony went on to explain his plans of moving to Oakland with his family, searching for a new purpose in life. He confided in me, "It's more than just money, you know? It's pretty much every area. Like, I love my wife, but sometimes we fight over stupid things, and I hold grudges against her. It's not easy to let go. It's my kids; I want to have more patience with them and not always get irritated when I come home from work. And it's my job; I want to earn more, but I'm not in a financial position to go back to school right now. We have two kids and one on the way. How could I ever find time to raise three kids, juggle a job, and pursue an education? I just don't see that happening. Do you have any advice for me? Because from what you've told me, it seems like you've got it all together. I want to have my life together too."

With empathy and sincerity, I offered Anthony three pieces of advice:

- *Focus on your family — but don't neglect yourself.* Your family is your anchor, and they depend on you. Prioritize them above all else. But remember, just as you are their rock, you need to focus on yourself as well.
- *Engage in education and self-improvement.* Explore online courses and certifications. You don't always need traditional schooling to acquire new skills. This can open doors to better career opportunities.
- *Practice self-care and nurture emotional well-being.* Taking care of yourself is essential. Allocate time for self-care and relaxation. This will help you manage your anger, frustration, and irritability.

Our conversation continued throughout the flight, and Anthony ultimately asked me a life-changing question: "Would you consider mentoring me? I value your insights, and I believe I need ongoing guidance for personal growth. Are you accepting clients?"

This unexpected request marked a turning point. As Anthony and I embarked on our coaching journey, I transitioned from Chloe the Consultant to Chloe the Coach. It became clear that my calling was to guide and support individuals like Anthony on their life paths.

This experience taught me that when we extend a helping hand and share our wisdom, the Universe rewards us in unexpected and profound ways. Guided by the Universe's subtle cues, I shifted my path and embraced my new role as a coach, ready to make a positive impact on the lives of others.

When we *believe* that everything will truly work out for us and we *expect* everything to work out for us, that is where the real magic lies.

Because that's when everything *does* work out for us.

MAGIC ACTION

Clarity on Overcoming Obstacles and Blocks

For this Magic Action, I want you to review some important tips from this chapter — especially if you are struggling in some area in your life and you need to remove blocks to get closer to your goal.

- *Don't try to get over on people — it will come back to you.* Remember that just as there is unlimited air to breathe, there are unlimited possibilities and abundance for all. You don't have to cheat, lie, misinform, or steal to have what you want.
- *When you do things from a place of love, we all win.* We live in a collective where everyone is affected by every decision that we make. A war between two countries affects the entire world. A school shooting affects so many people, not only those who send their children to school but others who may become afraid to sit in a movie theater or go to the grocery store. In our lifetimes we've already experienced enough drama to fill up multiple worlds for an eternity. Let your change in this world be a positive one.
- *Stop letting other folks make decisions for you.* You're a grown-ass person. (Well, you never know, you could be my teenaged nephew, and for that, sorry for cussing.) But anyways, let *you* be the judge of your life and decide what you want to do. Don't let others who have a lack mentality rub off on you. Their shortcomings are not your own. If you're unsure if a belief is yours or not, ask yourself, *Is this mine?* and ask it often. Because nine times out of ten, it isn't. It will help you discover that a lot of beliefs you've carried are actually other people's beliefs that you've been conditioned to adhere to but have nothing to do with your own. Release those beliefs and figure out your own.

- *Be afraid of your dreams — but dare to live them.* A lot of times we get so caught up in daydreaming about the life we shoulda, woulda, coulda had if only [*insert lame-ass excuse here*]. The truth of the matter is, we were just too scared to see if the life we really wanted would actually come true. Be scared of your dreams and conquer them anyway. Even if you only get halfway there, isn't it better than not moving in the direction of your dreams at all? Think about what steps to take, and do what you need to do to get there.

Chapter 16

Dancing with the Universe

We don't have to do all of it alone.
We were never meant to.

— BRENÉ BROWN, Renowned Research Professor,
New York Times Bestselling Author and Storyteller

When I first started co-creating with the Universe, I didn't know what I was doing. When things just started to work out for me, I would rejoice and savor them because I felt lucky that finally something good was happening to me. It wasn't until later in my life that I realized what I was doing was dancing with the Universe.

When we work with outside forces that are greater than ourselves, we try to understand what's going to happen, and we try to control the situation.

Please, God, gimme that promotion I'm up for, and I swear Imma start going to church every Sunday.

Please, God, let me get through this surgery. Imma stop eating so much fried chicken, I swear! I'm begging you, please!

Please, Lord, don't let her find out where I really was last night, oh Gawd have mercy. I'm going to change if I just make it through this.

We beg and plead because we don't know what else to do.

But what if instead we simply worked together with Source and asked for what we wanted? What if we just asked and then surrendered? I think a lot of times we lose sight of co-creation, and we just think about how badly we need things to work out for us. But how has it been working for you when you ask for things in desperation? Do you feel that you are always grasping at straws for things to happen, and as quickly as they come, they disappear? This is because you aren't co-creating with the Universe, but simply pleading for something to happen.

That's not how this thing works.

I remember one time in Detroit, I was getting my makeup done by a young lady who had recently started her own makeup business. She did an amazing job, and I paid her electronically through one of the cash apps and told her it was sent. She sent me frantic messages: "It's not coming through! It hasn't come through! Girl, you didn't send it!" A few minutes later, the money was in her account, but her panicky behavior was heartbreaking to me. She wasn't co-creating with the Universe and trusting that everything would work out for her. She had a lack of trust when it came to her clients, but also she probably had some experiences where she didn't believe that what was coming to her was coming to her. She was a prime example of the desperation we can feel when we don't trust ourselves or the Universe to come through for us.

Yet when we surrender and trust, everything we want comes to fruition. The Universe knows what you want, because you've asked for it, and it's going to bring it to you once you've reached the same frequency as the thing it is that you want. As I've said before, I know you want that million dollars...but are you matching the frequency level of that million dollars? If not, you already know what to do to make that your reality.

A lot of times we look for validation from others before we give ourselves permission to be who we really want to be.

Sometimes we figure that if we get the blessing from *them*, then it's all right to do what it is we think we should be doing. An important practice that I want you to learn at the end of this chapter is called "Stepping into Your Authentic Self." It allows you to dig deep within yourself and create personalized affirmations to fully embody your most essential qualities.

When my Grumma was living in a senior apartment some years before she died, we took a road trip to Chicago. I was interviewing for a job, and I thought it'd be nice for Grumma to tag along. We'd make it a girls' trip. We drove the four hours to Chicago, pulled up in the posh neighborhood of River North, and spent quality time talking, with her reminiscing about her younger years. I appreciated how she always encouraged me to chase my dreams. At the time, my dream wasn't to live in Chicago — it was just to get out of Detroit. I needed a new experience, and I needed a new place to expand into the Chloe I was meant to be — my Authentic Self.

Well, I didn't get that job in Chicago — and I see now that it was because it wasn't the place for me. Unconsciously, I had asked the Universe to help me catapult my career with a higher-paying job so I could re-create myself. I wanted to expand, but I just didn't know *how* to at this point in my life. I didn't care if my new job was in Chicago or anywhere else in the country — I just knew that I wanted new experiences. I'd thrown this out there to the Universe, and the Universe had something better in mind than that job in Chicago. The Universe came and said to me, *You know what, Clo? How about we get you a higher-paying job, still out of state, but one that's even better than the one you interviewed for?* And a few weeks later, I landed my high-paying job in Indiana.

When we are open to expansion while co-creating with the Universe, the Universe will bring things to us that we may not have imagined before. Things we cannot yet see. It may not be in exactly the form we asked for — it can be something even better.

That job in Indiana catapulted me to meet my then boyfriend, now husband, which then expanded me to move from Indiana back to Detroit, and then from Detroit to California, which then expanded me to doing even bigger and better things. Do you catch my drift? This is the magic when we co-create with the Universe.

Going back to the time when I got the job in Indiana, that experience shook me to my core. For the first time in my life, everything was going right for me. I had a high-paying job, an amazing group of friends, my dream luxury apartment, my dream car, my dream man. It had all snowballed to me. I became expansive. I had developed this new ability to trust my gut, which was also part of my expansion. When you're working with expansion and you begin living as your Authentic Self, you will notice synchronicities, signs, intuition, gut feelings, and pings that are the Universe's way of alerting you to pay attention to something in your life.

It is OK to accept what we cannot change
and to change what we can.

When you're starting to trust your intuition and co-create with the Universe, it can be scary — especially when your mind is telling you one thing but your gut is insisting that it knows better. I get it, I totally do. But when we take a chance and choose faith over fear, we live a fruitful life. We venture through our journey, we learn the lessons life is trying to teach us, and we end up really enjoying the life we're living. As I've mentioned time and time again, life doesn't have to be hard. You can *choose* to be happy today.

Let's try it.

Curve your mouth in an upward motion.

Show some teeth.

Sit in it ... for five ... four ... three ... two ... one.

Smile!

Laugh!

Because at the end of the day, this experience we're living on earth is what we make of it. So why not make it a great one? Whenever I have a moment when I'm not feeling at my best, I just smile. I shake whatever I was feeling off of me, and I let it move on by. I acknowledge it, but I don't sit and dwell in it. It's taken me a lot of time — and practice makes perfect — but when we can be silly with ourselves, we really can live a happier and healthier life.

Everything will always work out for you.

That's my mantra for you.

But back to the Universe.

So anyway. Co-creating.

When you work with the Universe to co-create your life, it's like dancing with a partner who knows all the steps. Trust the flow, let go, and allow yourself to be led by a beautiful musical masterpiece you create together.

When we step out of fear and into our Authentic Self, that is when the real magic happens. The right people reach out to you from seemingly nowhere. Things start falling in place. You feel like you're finally on your path. You start to trust yourself and your gut.

Now you might be saying, *But what if things don't start working out for me, Clo? Then what am I supposed to do?* Sometimes, when something big is about to happen in your life, you may feel one or two or three things (we're all different).

You may feel like the shit has hit the fan, and you don't know what to do. OK, let's go to work. If you feel like there is a roadblock between you and your dreams, it could be a sign that your manifestation is almost complete and the Universe is asking you if you're really ready for it. *Is this what you really, really want?*

I recall a time when a friend asked me if I thought she should marry her partner — on the day of her wedding. I was taken aback because if you've come this far, anything other than "I do" turns into a Lifetime movie. But I digress. I told her to dig deep into her Authentic Self and ask herself, was this what she really wanted? Was this the partner she was calling in? Did he have all the essences she wanted in a partner? Or was intergenerational expectation of what a woman should do and when she should do it rearing its ugly head?

You have to be 100 percent clear and certain that if the thing you want comes true, it's really what you want. Not something you "should" get or something you think you "should" have at this time in your life, but *exactly* what you want or better. So if a roadblock comes up in your life, be prepared to either (a) overcome it or (b) re-evaluate your Authentic Self to make sure this is really what you want. If it isn't, then you know you have inner work to do to create the version of yourself that is true to you.

Oh, and my friend? Fast-forward to the present day. She is happily married to her guy, and they have three beautiful children together.

You also might feel like giving up. It's either because what you want feels like hard work, you're overexerting yourself, or you feel as if you bit off more than you could chew. If this is the case, you need to take a step back and re-evaluate your strategy. It also means that the thing you want is still at a much higher vibrational frequency level than where you are. Ask yourself a couple of things:

- *Am I trying to do more than I can sustain?* If your goal is to lose weight and you haven't been to the gym in over a year, deciding to go to the gym six days a week will last only on willpower — which is not a long-term sustainable solution. As soon as you get to week two on your gym plan, your body may be physically exhausted, and you won't feel like going to the gym ever again.

Instead, you need to build up your inner power, which will more than outlast your willpower, because your inner strength comes from your Authentic Self (who you are becoming, a person who regularly goes to the gym). This may mean starting off by going to the gym two days a week and re-evaluating the goal after you've stabilized that habit.

- *Am I doing anything at all?* Some of us have a problem with procrastination. We know what we need to do to get where we wanna go, but guess what? We don't wanna do it! It's not out of sheer laziness; it is just that the thing that we want is looking like an eight-hundred-pound gorilla, and we don't know how to tackle it. So instead of taking baby steps around the big thing, we try to jump on its back, and it throws us off. We are so scared of being thrown off of the gorilla for a second time (as it might be the last) that we say, "Fluck this shite" and just sit and have a staring contest with it.

  This is not how it works, folks. We, as humans living on this planet, must work with the universal laws of this world. With that being said, we have to do the work to get where we gotta go. Otherwise, we won't get past that gorilla who is blocking us from our dream, and we'll procrastinate for the rest of our lives...until we decide to change.

It can definitely feel scary, sure. But it also means that the thing we want on the other side of that gorilla is operating at a much higher vibrational frequency level than where we are currently at. In order to raise our vibe to get where we want to go, we need to take small steps around the gorilla. This may mean getting up thirty minutes earlier than usual to hit the gym. This may mean making five additional phone calls a day to pitch your idea to investors. This may mean prepping your food for the week on a Sunday so you aren't frazzled and hangry when it's time to eat. This may mean no more fried foods for dinner every night so you can get off your insulin. This may mean putting away an additional 10 percent of your paycheck to save up to buy that property you've had your eye on. This may mean writing for an hour a day to finish your book. Whatever you need to do, you need to take small steps so it isn't overwhelming. Small daily steps lead to daily wins. Daily wins lead to momentum to keep going. Momentum leads to you carving out your Authentic Self and stepping into your power. You got this! And before you know it, you look up and you're at your goal.

Finally, maybe you're exhausted from trying. Have you just said, "This is too hard for me — I really need time off"? Take the time off you need and then come back to re-evaluate. You don't have to go, go, go, go, go. Give yourself permission to just *be*. It's OK to simply sit in peace, do nothing, and enjoy it. You deserve a break. In those moments, we can truly craft our Authentic Self and come back stronger than before.

Stepping into Your Authentic Self

Our Authentic Self is the person we were born to be — whole, unscathed, and pure. It is who we were before beliefs were instilled in us, when nothing could deter us from life. We just were. We were living in each precious moment, just being. We were whole and full of life.

As time went on, those who raised us instilled their values and beliefs in us. Those values and beliefs became our own, tainting our world and creating feelings in us we had not known before. Fear. Unworthiness. Shame. Doubt. Insecurity. Guilt. Worry. Lack. All these feelings and so many more have shaped the life we're living today.

Getting back to your Authentic Self means re-creating the

you you were always meant to be. You are already whole, but the world you live in may have tainted that image for you, and your perception of who you really are may have faltered. You may not believe you are beautiful or worthy or capable or strong or protected or safe. Whatever limiting beliefs you have are not your fault. It is time to come back to self. Your Authentic Self. *Whole. Full. Rich. Vibrant. Safe. Protected. Abundant. Worthy. Beautiful. Strong. Loved. Uniquely you.*

MAGIC MOMENT
Customized Authentic Self Affirmations

Reflect on your childhood, a time of innocence and pure authenticity. Recall the qualities of your childhood self — how you were during that time in your life. Think about how you would describe yourself then — maybe you were funny, sassy, brave, smart, or kind.

Now I want you to create your own affirmation that embodies these qualities. For example:

- *I embrace my innate qualities — my courage, humor, intelligence, and creativity. These traits are the foundation of my True Self, and I am on a journey to manifest my limitless life.*
- *I celebrate my intrinsic virtues, and I am embarking on a path to manifest my ideal life.*
- *I am so in love with my Authentic Self. I celebrate all that is me, knowing there is no other human being who possesses the same unique blend of qualities and experiences that I do.*
- *I am deserving of love and respect for being my Authentic Self.*
- *By being my True Self, I am a gift to the world, and I share it unapologetically.*

Repeat your mantra every day for the next week, noticing how you feel and how much more in tune you've become with knowing who you are and embracing your Authentic Self.

When you step into the power of your Authentic Self, no one can bring you down. You are a powerful, unstoppable force; you know where you're going and how you're going to get there. You are in full co-creation mode with the Universe, and your every desire is the Universe's command. When you step into your Authentic Self, everything just clicks. Everything on every level is in perfect formation, falling into place for you. Everything. And when everything works out for you, no one and nothing can take that away. It is your birthright to be a successful, abundant human being on this earth if only you choose to be so. That, of course, means taking action. Remember we talked about this back in chapter 7? Refer back to the Magical Magnetism Method if you need a refresher.

Chapter 17

Prosperity Magic

Successful people make money. It's not that people who make money become more successful, but that successful people attract money. They bring success to what they do.

— WAYNE DYER, American Author, Motivational Speaker, Native Detroiter

When it comes to co-creating with the Universe to attract money, your mind will always tell you it's going to be a billion times harder than it actually will be. This is because when you're trying to manifest from the ego versus your Authentic Self, your ego can get in the way. Your ego will tell you things like *It has to be done this way, or it won't work* or *If it's not done the way I'm telling you to do it, you're never gonna get what you want.*

In other words, the ego is very limited. If it isn't the ego's way, it's no way at all. The ego doesn't believe in magic or miracles. It believes in logic from our own experiences, not in anything beyond what we haven't already done or the possibilities of what can be done.

This is *not* how you want to manifest things. Yes, manifesting from the ego is very possible and can happen, but it closes you off to other possibilities that might have required less work, less stress, and fewer aligned actionable steps. Operating from your Authentic Self allows manifestations to freely flow. Operation from the egoistic self limits the way manifestations are attracted to you.

When you manifest through your Authentic Self, you are co-authoring with the Universe. The Universe in turn will then bring you unlimited possibilities through which your manifestations can happen. Whether you're manifesting a new life, a partner, a new career, or a new venture that will allow you to do what you love while earning what you want, when you consciously do it from your Authentic Self, you are being present. In this moment. Right now. Today.

To manifest money and the life that you want, you have to reprogram your way of thinking to repel what it is that you don't want and attract what it is that you do. The reason some of us lack money is because we need to do some reprogramming to reverse situations, memories, or experiences that aren't serving us in our lives. In order to reprogram ourselves to attract abundance, we can do a few things to help us get to the root cause and rewire the way that we think. But first you might be thinking, *How do I know if I need to reprogram myself to manifest money into my life?* Do any of the following apply to you?

- You live in lack.
- You're broke.
- You've just lost your job or a stream of income.
- You're not happy in your job or career.
- You keep repeating situations in a loop because you're fearful of what to do next.
- You're financially set, and you don't know what to do next.

If you're experiencing any of these states, keep reading to find out how to reprogram your way of thinking.

What Is Money, Really?

As I've said before, money is really energy, when you think about it. We need it to survive, live our lives, have fun, feel safe and secure, and live comfortably and beyond in this world. Money is not evil, not the devil, and not "bad," whatever that means. It just *is*. It is energy, and how much we have expands or contracts with our self-worth.

This is why it is so important to step fully into our Authentic Self, as this is when we are truly expanded, and the more expanded we become, the more we allow the flow of money into our lives. The Universe will shower down on us all the abundance we believe we deserve. We have to remember that we do not manifest money through our thoughts. Just thinking about money does not make it come. We manifest (or repel) money through our subconscious beliefs that have been deeply instilled in us from childhood, adolescence, and even as adults. Our ability to manifest it is simply based on our own self-worth.

By the end of this chapter, you should have a strong understanding of how much or how little you are aligned with your Authentic Self and your own self-worth around money. If you grew up in a poor household, your subconscious thoughts around money may be bleak. You may be unintentionally sabotaging your self-worth if it has been instilled in you since childhood that money is scarce, there isn't enough for everyone, and you have to either work extremely hard in a job you don't like or lie, cheat, or steal in order to get it.

For us to up-level our relationship with money, we first must reprogram the way we think about money. This means we have to go back to our childhood and think about all the times we felt we weren't deserving of something, didn't receive something we wanted, or were told we couldn't have something because of a lack of money. We might also need to examine experiences we had seeing the adults in our lives mismanage money, experiences our subconscious may have taken in as our own. Let's undo all that work.

What Is Lack Mentality, and Do You Have It?

Lack mentality is when you don't feel deserving or worthy of having something. Lack comes from experiences that stem from your childhood and generated feelings of shame, pain, and unworthiness in you. If you've never experienced what was possible for you to have at a young age (for instance, being a successful Black woman under the age of thirty running a billion-dollar company), you may feel it is impossible for you to aspire to.

When manifesting money, we have to understand that it isn't 100 percent up to us to decide on what we get. The Universe co-creates with us to help us expand our horizons and gently reminds us that the heavy lifting will be done mostly by a force greater than ourselves. We have to learn to let go and be OK with receiving something that may be outside of what we asked for but vastly better than what we consciously wanted. Let's say you're working on manifesting a higher-paying career, but deep down what you really want is to have a more relaxed job with little to no stress and still make more money than what you currently make. But you lack the belief that your career life doesn't have to be stressful. You don't feel deserving of a career that is low stress and high paying. You think that asking for a higher-paying career will cause you more stress, but you lie to yourself and say you're OK with this tradeoff for more money. This limiting belief could stem from childhood experiences where adults in your life worked extremely hard and were stressed in order to achieve success. The message you took in was: *More money = more problems.*

But what if the Universe wants to bring you a higher-paying role with *virtually zero stress*? You'll get the best bang for your manifesting buck when you allow the Universe to co-create with you and you surrender to the idea that rather than getting exactly what you've asked for, the Universe will bring you the *essence* of it and that it will be equal to or greater than what you said you wanted. If you want to attract more money, you have to ask yourself, *Do I already feel abundant? Or do I feel broke and stressed and limited in the things I can do?* If your thoughts are aligned with lack, you will only bring more lack into your life. If your thoughts are not aligned with the money, the money won't come.

When you manifest from your Authentic Self, your thoughts and emotions are aligned with what you want. Even if you don't have it yet, you need to act like you have abundance. You need to act and feel as if you are already living an amazing life. This is how you bring more moolah to you. If you act from feelings of brokenness, the Universe will only bring more of that to you, because that is the energy level you are operating on. Lower thought energetics will only bring you more lower thought energetics. When you operate from your higher thought energetics, you are going to attract more love, abundance, health, and joy. All the good things are gonna continuously come your way.

Now you may be wondering, *How do I just ask for something and then let it go? How is it going to happen for me? Shouldn't I hold on tight to what I want? When will I know that what I've asked for is really gonna come?* And I'm going to tell you that when you surrender to the Universe, the Universe will work on the how and when for you. You just have to let go, trust in a Source that is greater than yourself, and know that everything will work out for you. As scary as that may sound, you just have to do it. I've done this countless times, and every time I surrender and trust the process, everything always works out in my favor. I can't tell you the things I've manifested just by simply surrendering. When you've done things so many times that haven't worked, you become open to trying new things that will.

Now please don't confuse "surrendering" with "no action." Surrendering is when you've done the work, and you are simply putting your trust in the Universe to bring forth what you want. Work still must be done. In order to get anything in this life, you need to take action.

My friend Harper was up for a promotion at her job. She desperately wanted to be a director in her company, and she spent a year prepping for her dream role, hoping that one day a director role would open up. Finally, her dream job was posted, she applied, and the day came for the final interviews. She told me on the phone that she just "had to have this role," she "desperately" needed it, and she didn't know what she'd do if she didn't get it.

I told her to surrender and just say to herself, *If I don't get it, it's OK because it means something better is on the way.* She said that type of thinking didn't work for her and she had to do anything and everything in her power to land this role. I wished her well.

A few days later, I called her to see how she was doing. She started crying and told me that she was passed up for another woman who hadn't done nearly as much of the prep work as she had.

I asked her, "How do you know she didn't do as much work to land the promotion?"

"Because homegirl said, and I quote, 'If it's meant to be my role, it will be,' with a certain detachment about the whole thing. Girl, the nerve!" She sounded hysterical.

"Why was that so bad? Why does it mean she didn't do any work?"

"Who says that and then lands a promotion, Chloe? Nobody, girl! I don't know what fantasy world you living in, but in the real world, people need jobs. Good-paying ones if you wanna live a good life out here in these streets." I imagined her rolling her eyes and tossing her hair back as she said it.

"That woman did," I said, probably a little too bluntly. "Listen. Just because *you* think she didn't do anything doesn't mean she didn't put in the work. She did exactly what I told you to do, and you didn't. She wasn't clawing for it for dear life. She surrendered it, and she got it. I know it can be a tough pill to swallow, but those are facts." She was silent as I let my last statement sink in. "Maybe next time, don't be so clingy. You've done the work; you're a smart girl. Next time, be like your co-worker and have 'a certain detachment to it,'" I said with a fake British accent. That got her laughing.

"Will do, Clo. Will do."

A couple of months later, Harper landed her dream role. She was hired to be executive director at a new company, where she's earning even more than the other position would have offered her. When she finally learned to surrender, all types of wonderful things began to happen to her.

When the Universe works on our behalf, we don't have to worry about the how. The Universe works diligently in our favor when we let go. But just because we don't have to worry about the *how* part doesn't mean we're off the hook when it comes to taking aligned action. When you are consciously present in your life, you will be called to do actionable items that are aligned with what you are calling in. These are the steps you need to take to get closer to your manifestation. I'll use Harper as an example. Because she was working from her ego, she spent a year feverishly doing things that were going against her Authentic Self. If she had worked from her Authentic Self from the beginning, her year of hard work could have been eliminated, as she would have been called to take aligned actionable steps instead of ego-driven action.

Understanding How to Co-create with the Universe to Attract Money

Some of us feel that we have to hold a certain intention in order to get what we want. And while there is nothing wrong with that, you have to understand first if this intention is really what your Authentic Self wants or if this is coming from your ego self.

Here's how to tell the difference.

Ask yourself: *Is what I'm calling in coming from the ego?*

When we manifest from the ego, it will feel hard and challenging. It will feel as if there is a force keeping you from having it. A long, hard journey to the top. When you try to make things happen, like Harper did, you're stuck in your head. You have only your thoughts and logic and past experiences to help you figure things out. You aren't present in the moment; you're constantly searching for a way to make it work. When you're not present, you miss opportunities that offer themselves to you to make what it is you want your reality. If this describes your process, you're trying to manifest from the ego.

Ask yourself: *Is what I'm calling in coming from my Authentic Self?*

When you co-create with the Universe, you are manifesting from your Authentic Self. You are present in the moment, and you are open and receptive to new ways of thinking and attracting what you want. It feels easy, breezy, beautiful, Cover-Girl. (Naw, I'm just kidding. I loved those commercials.) But seriously. It will feel easy, breezy, and flowy. You've set your intentions, you have aligned your thoughts to match those of the high vibrational frequency level of the thing it is that you want, and you know it's coming to you. You have taken the aligned actionable steps, and you know the Universe is co-creating with you to make it yours. You feel peaceful and calm knowing that it will come. If this describes your process, you are manifesting from your Authentic Self.

Remember, you aren't setting an intention to bring in more money — your intention should be set to attract the *essence* of what having money allows you to do. Is it being able to stay a week at the Ritz-Carlton on a whim, just because? Is it being able to invest in real estate and build generational wealth for yourself and your family? Is it being able to buy sustainable luxury items because they make you feel good and you're also conscious of your carbon footprint? Is it being able to do absolutely nothing and feel great about it? Is it being able to go on a yoga retreat and get back to nature? Call in the essence, *not* the money.

If you're trying to manifest money from a place of lack, know that the Universe will only bring you more lack — not money. Your intentions should always be focused on the core essence of the thing it is that you want. Please stop thinking about what you don't have. Moping around, crying, and complaining to other folks about how things are not working out for you are *not* going to bring you closer to manifesting what you want. Believe me, I tried that for years, and during those years I was broker than broke. That way of thinking just doesn't work. In order for this to work, you have to start thinking about the essence of what you want in this life. The money is simply a tool for having that thing. If you want to splurge on a week-long vacation at the Ritz-Carlton because it makes you feel good, you are calling in the essence of luxury and serenity. Know that the Universe will work in your favor to bring you that experience or something better. If you want to just enjoy a quiet life, full of joyful moments and pleasantries, you are calling in the essence of bliss. Focus on the essences of what you desire, and your manifestations will come.

Use the Magic Action list below to help you set your intentions for creating and attracting money into your life.

MAGIC ACTION

Creating Your Dream Financial Future

1. Set your intention for what it is that you really want money to provide for you, coming from your Authentic Self. Let's say, for example, you want financial abundance because it will allow you to create a peaceful retreat in nature, where you can find harmony and reconnect with your inner self whenever you need.

2. Focus on that essence and the feeling of having money. What does it feel like to have serenity in your life? Focus on that feeling.

3. Take the aligned actionable steps.

4. Co-create with the Universe to bring to you what it is that you want. This means you do your part (setting your intention, focusing on the essence of your desired manifestation, doing the aligned actionable steps) and let the Universe do the rest. Remember, the Universe works in ways that are greater than our understanding. We leave the *how* part (*How is this going to work for me?*) up to a Source greater than us. This is how miracles happen and how manifestations can seem like magic. Let the *how* part unfold right before your eyes. Trust in the process.

5. Sit back and enjoy your life as your manifestation comes to you.

Chapter 18

Calling In Love

Your task is not to seek love, but merely to seek and find all the barriers within yourself that you have built against it.

— Rumi, Thirteenth-Century Sufi Poet,
Master of Words, Islamic Scholar

I remember a time in my early twenties when I went to a strip club with my friends, and a woman proceeded to the stage to drop a set of — from the looks of it — luxury car keys inside a half-naked man's crotch. While everyone was whooping and hollering and carrying on, I sat there with a puzzled look, wondering what had possessed this woman to buy this man a car. Maybe she was extremely wealthy and had it like that. Maybe *she too* had a luxury car — a Benz or a Rolls or something of the sort — but her being in a male strip club in the hood on the east side of Detroit gave me my doubts about her financial stability.

As we proceeded to go outside and admire the car, which turned out to be a Jag, I couldn't help but notice one of my friends snickering.

"What's so funny?" I asked her as she covered her laugh with her hands.

"Nothing, Clo," she said slyly, doubling over uncontrollably.

"Bitch, if you don't tell me…" I said with my hands on my

hips. Strip clubs were not my choice of entertainment. "Got me out here looking crazy in this place. I'm getting ready to go home."

"OK! OK!" She pulled me into a hug. "It's just funny because...because...*he's* gonna be taking me out in it tomorrow night. She thinks he's out here being faithful 'cuz she bought him a Jag, but little do she know..." She proceeded to look up and down at the girl, who was all over her man.

"You mean the Jag?" I did a double take. "I don't even know why you mess with dudes like this. I mean, he's a stripper. How could he be faithful to anybody when he can get it for free so easily? Or have women take care of him? He'll just tell you what you wanna hear, just like he's gonna lie to that girl when he takes you out tomorrow night. 'Nah, baby, it ain't like that. She's just a fan, know what I'm saying? Just another girl from the club.'"

"Girl, he is fine as hell. That's why I mess with him. And he got money."

"And this is what you call sustainability? How many male strippers do you know over the age of thirty? Stripping isn't some long-term career goal. OK, girl. You do you. I'm gonna roll up on outta here. Don't wanna be on the east side too late at night anyway." I hugged my friend goodbye and skedaddled out of that place.

We don't have to buy love or persuade others to love us. That's not how this thing works. Love is a two-way street, and it is reciprocated both ways. When we are calling in love, we are calling in something that is equal to what we are already emitting into the world. If we feel we need to take drastic measures to gain the attention of others or do outlandish things to convince them that we are the one, we will only push that person further away from us — and we have a lot of deep inner work to do ourselves.

I don't need to tell you how the end of the story went with my old friend. You can pretty much figure it out. The woman who bought the man a Jag eventually found out he wasn't faithful to her and took the Jag back. My friend, on the other hand, convinced that he wouldn't cheat on *her*, stayed with him up until the point that he got her pregnant — *and* got three other women pregnant at the same damn time. This isn't a happy story.

As you can guess, my friend didn't know her worth. Her mother had men who came in and out of her life all the time. All cheaters and deadbeats. Every other weekend, she'd tell me a story about her momma and her new man and what kind of car he drove. That was her measure of success: the type of car a man drove. On a subconscious level my friend felt as if she, too, could only attract these unreliable types of men — and so she did. Instead of trying to change within herself, she always tried to change the man. Who we know we can't change. We can't change anybody. Little did my friend know that the company she kept was attracted to her because of the frequency she was operating on: scarcity, unworthiness, shame, doubt, and fear. Because, on an ego level, she believed she deserved a certain type of man, she didn't dig deep within herself to attract the type of man her whole Authentic Self desired and deserved. She didn't believe this type of man existed.

When we are attracting love, we are attracting from a subconscious level. If we have unresolved trauma or are still saying, "Men ain't shit," well, then, we're only going to attract shitty folks into our lives. If you believe your body size or car or job or some other excuse is a factor, the people you date will pick up on that energy and make it a big deal because you do. Ever notice when you go on a date or meet someone for the first time that your insecurity is one of the first things they detect? They may not say it to your face, but it eventually becomes the cause of why things didn't work out.

Take my friend Mitchell. He believed that because he was a heavyset guy, women wouldn't be attracted to him. He'd go out on dates, but afterward, he wouldn't hear from the women again. He would tell me that the women he dated said things like "You're a lot bigger than your photos!" or "I can tell you love a home-cooked meal!" or "You look like Michael B. Jordan if he was about seventy pounds heavier." Mitchell just didn't know why he couldn't attract a woman who wouldn't care about his weight. He was trying to get healthier, yes, and had already lost thirty pounds, but they didn't know that and wouldn't give him the time of day. Because he was focusing on his insecurities, he attracted women who also focused on those insecurities. Had he been focusing on the qualities and the essence of what he wanted a woman to bring to the table instead, he would have had more success with dating.

After I helped him through some inner work, Mitchell decided to give dating a try again *without* focusing on his insecurities. And since he was so flattered by the Michael B. Jordan insult/compliment, I asked him what would he do if he *was* Michael B. Jordan? How would he go about his day? He said he'd work out, of course, because he's got to stay in shape. He'd eat right, be sure of himself. He'd have no issue with attracting the right woman because he was a high-quality man.

"Then act like it," I said to Mitchell over the phone.

"You know what, Clo? You're right. Nothing else has worked. I'm going to give this a shot."

"That's right. Tomorrow morning, we're hitting the gym bright and early, and you will become Mr. Michael B. Jordan. That confidence. That demeanor. That's the new you for thirty days, OK? Just trust me on this one. Do this for thirty days. If you don't like it, you can go back to the old you. Deal?"

"Deal."

For the next thirty days, Mitch and I proceeded to hit the

gym in the morning to help him get into form. He ate clean, healthy foods. When he looked in the mirror, he saw the confident man that he wanted to become who didn't think about his weight because it was irrelevant. By day twenty-five, Mitch had dropped eighteen pounds. I no longer needed to hold his hand at the gym. A woman who also worked out there came up to me and asked if we were together. I told her he was my friend and he was on the market. She went over to him and said she was impressed with his progress and *asked him out*. Needless to say, Mitch has continued to grow, and the last time we talked, he and his new girlfriend from the gym were going strong.

Mitch got over his insecurity of being overweight by taking the aligned action to remove the insecurity from his life. He was ready for transformation, and he was ready for love. This worked out in Mitch's favor because he not only stepped into his Authentic Self, but he was open and receptive to creating change (by us going to the gym to help him get over his insecurity).

How to Work on the Subconscious Level to Attract Love

In order to attract the person you want in your life, you have to do the inner work first — that is, working on the subconscious level to remove any blocks that are keeping you stuck in your love life. This is the only way to operate from your Authentic Self and attract sustainable love.

You first have to remove emotional baggage and trauma from past relationships. You do this by following the Magic Actions at the end of chapter 13. Once you've cleared blockages and have done the necessary inner work, you can then allow in abundance, attracting the partner you truly desire. The partner of your dreams *can* be yours — you just have to be aligned with your Authentic Self in order to receive them.

Once you've done the inner work and cleared your emotional baggage and trauma from previous relationships, you can work on visualizing your ideal partner. You can visualize any aspect of them, from their physical qualities to the way they behave around others to how they will treat you and what a life with them would be like. Write down the qualities, essence, and appearance of what you want from your partner. Vividly describe them. What color is their hair? (Maybe they don't have hair, and that's fine too.) How do they dress? What's their build? What's the color of their skin? How do they treat you? How do they react in uncomfortable situations? Are they comforting to you when you're feeling down? How do they help to uplift you? All these questions and more need to be thought about and answered.

You also have to ask yourself, *If the partner of my dreams showed up in front of me and I was physically attracted to them, but they lacked all the other qualities I want, would this still be my ideal partner?* Absolutely not. If they are lacking the key essences you're calling in, they are not your person. Warning: If such a person shows up, this is the Universe testing you to see if what you're asking for is what you really, really want. Don't fail this test! Don't fall for these folks who aren't meeting you halfway. If you do date this person who doesn't meet your qualifications, you are pushing your manifestation further away. You are telling the Universe, *I'm going to settle for less. I don't really want what I told you I really, really want. Thanks anyway.* Don't fall for it. Wait a bit. Your person is just around the corner.

Stop doubting yourself. You deserve love, and love deserves you. Many of us feel that we are undeserving of love. As if we're past our prime or too this or too that for love to come our way. Those beliefs only push love further away from us. As I've mentioned time and time again throughout this book, our thoughts become things because we believe in them so much. They are what we tell our subconscious mind we feel we deserve.

If you really feel you're too old for love and that you'll never have it, then guess what? You won't. It isn't until you stop self-sabotaging that love will come your way.

I remember a story of an elderly woman who thought she'd never find love again after her husband died. For twenty years, she kept telling herself she was too old for companionship. One day, she said, "You know what? Too old or not, I'm still here, and I want companionship." Out of the blue, she received a letter from her first love, who had gone away to fight in World War II and disappeared. They were supposed to get married, but she'd moved on after five years of searching for him. It turns out that someone had stolen his identity in the war. After all these years, he found her and wrote her asking if it was too late. She was elated. They became husband and wife and lived together until they both passed away peacefully in their sleep. It was because she felt deserving of love that this out-of-the-blue letter landed on her doorstep. There are no coincidences. It is simply the Universe working in our favor when we are open and ready to receive. When you tell yourself, *I am open to love* and *I am deserving of love*, love comes your way.

Take care of yourself. When you practice self-love, you are sending out love to the world and, by doing so, attracting what you desire. You're also preparing to be an amazing partner to what you're calling in. Self-care could be as simple as exercising on a regular basis. Going for walks in nature. Respecting yourself and others. Loving yourself no matter where you are on your journey of love. Nourishing your body at every meal with whole, delicious plant foods, such as vegetables and fruits. When you respect yourself, you attract others who are vibrating at the same level as you: partners who respect themselves, love themselves, and are happy, open, and receptive to love.

When you do the inner work, it reflects on the outside. Take, for instance, me when I was calling in my husband. Before I called him in, I had work to do on myself, because the caliber of man I wanted wasn't at the energy level I was operating on at that time in my life. I didn't want a broke man or someone who was unstable. I didn't want a man who couldn't control his emotions or someone who felt anger all the time because of what he lacked in life. I wanted the opposite of all that. I wanted someone who was financially fit, genuine, and a slew of other qualities. But I also knew that in order to call him in, I needed to have myself together to match the vibrational frequency level of what I wanted.

I wanted to be in shape and lose some weight, so I started working out regularly and fell in love with running. I lost sixty-five pounds in the process of being active and eating lots of vegetables and fruits. My finances weren't in order, so I started to pay off my debt. I needed to make more money because my Authentic Self demanded a higher salary to live the lifestyle of my dreams, so I called in a higher-paying job. I wanted to live in a lavish apartment, so I called in a luxury apartment I was able to afford because I was bringing in a higher salary and had improved my credit. I wanted to look and feel good, so after losing weight, I changed my entire wardrobe to clothes that fit me well. I found confidence in myself that wasn't there before. I started to smile more, and I became happier just because I loved myself so much more.

My friends noticed how much I glowed and how much I changed. How much better I looked. So did my family. I was becoming my Authentic Self. I was at a place where I felt I was finally ready to call in love. And I called him in, and he came. In order to get what we want, we must do the work. Calling in a new man doesn't require hoping and wishing and pleading — it requires aligned action. Once you are aligned with your Authentic Self, you will know what you need to do to get where you want to go.

You may also already be in the process of doing the aligned actionable steps to call in your person. That's amazing! But it will take time. Once you surrender to a power greater than yourself, that power will work in your favor by bringing to you what you want. You just have to believe that what you want *can be yours*, that it *already is yours*, and that it is only a matter of time before it shows itself to you. When I called in my husband, I knew he was already mine. I didn't know what he looked liked or when he would come, but I knew a life of added happiness was on the way — I just hadn't reached that moment in time yet. And sure enough, this happiness came through and has been amplified ever since. I didn't hold on tight and beg it not to go. A lot of times, we are so afraid that people will leave us that they actually do — because they weren't ours to begin with. We don't need to beg and plead for anyone to be with us.

Take my friend Janette. She was calling in a man to be a father to her two kids and a husband to her. Janette was doing her aligned actionable steps. She had joined a gym and lost some weight. She'd recently been promoted to a managerial role in her company, and she was doing well — but she refused to surrender. She met a few men on the dating apps, and as soon as the date was over, she'd text them and call them and talk to them and beg and plead for the next date. She didn't understand how letting something go would allow what she desired to come to her, and she was afraid to do it.

"Chill out with that, girl, let the man call you," I said one day while we were having brunch. "You don't have to come off so desperate, girl. You're good."

"Chloe, I have two kids, and I'm a divorcée. I have baggage. I have to let them know I'm interested." She took a sip of her mimosa, sat back in her seat, and sighed, looking toward the park beyond the outside terrace where we were dining.

"This isn't the 1950s, sweetie. Being a divorcée is hardly taboo. That clown ex-husband of yours didn't deserve you, girl, and you know it. You can't take care of two kids and a husband who refused to get a job after two years. Anybody in their right mind would have left him."

"But it's different now, Clo. I'm in my thirties, girl. I'm tired. I do a lot of running around after the kids. I need a partner, and my clock is running out. If my new man wanted to start a family, I'd still want to be able to give him a baby."

"I hear you," I said. "But it doesn't mean you need to act in desperation. Just surrender yourself. You put it out there, what you want. Just wait for it to come through." I took a sip of my chai while I examined her frazzled face. I knew she didn't like my answer; she looked at me as if I was speaking another language. "Tell you what," I said. "Why don't you keep doing what you're doing, acting all desperate and clinging to men like you need them, and see how that goes, OK? And then, once you're tired of men blocking your number because you nag them and they can smell your desperation from across town, come back to me and see how the surrendering strategy goes. It requires way less work, and we both know yo ass don't like to work much. So. How 'bout that?"

Janette snorted as she bellowed a laugh. "You know what? You got a smart mouth, Clo, but yo sarcastic ass is always up to something, and you usually right. Imma give it a try."

"OK, girl. We shall see."

Four months later, Janette was a completely new woman. She had this spark about her that I hadn't seen before, a new confidence. She was promoted again, this time to senior director, because of a project she pulled together that impressed the CEO. Her ex-husband finally got a job and was paying her alimony and child support. *And* she found a new man — one who was head over heels for her just the way that she was and loved her two little girls. Once Janette took my advice and surrendered, she deleted the dating apps from her phone and stopped calling and texting the guys who didn't add up to everything she wanted in a man. She became more interested in going to the gym and joined a spin class and happened to meet Kenneth, who was everything on her list and more and who is now her fiancé (congratulations, guys!). Though she was scared, she realized that what she was doing just wasn't working, and she decided that surrendering might be what the Universe was trying to get her to do after all. Her life couldn't be happier, and she's expecting a baby boy soon.

MAGIC MOMENT

Affirmations for Attracting Love

These affirmations have helped not only me but countless other people I have coached and mentored over the years to attract everlasting love. I encourage you to say them to yourself, whether aloud or in your mind when you have a moment of silence, and fully believe in their power to help you attract your perfect, ideal partner.

- *I am loved.*
- *I am deserving of love.*
- *I am worthy of love.*
- *I am love.*
- *I love myself unconditionally.*
- *I love myself for who I am right now.*
- *I am worth it.*

 GO EVEN DEEPER

Calling in love, creating self-love, and eliminating low self-worth take time. That's why I've created this Creative Imagining: to help you dive even deeper to heal yourself from past wounds and to love yourself on a profound and transformative level. Please go to my website to access your Creative Imagining audio: ChloePanta.co/um-6.

Chapter 19

Falling Out with Fear

To overcome the fear, here's all you have to do:
realize the fear is there, and do the action you fear anyway.

— PETER MCWILLIAMS, American Author, Native Detroiter,
Positive Thinking Influencer

When I was seventeen years old, I was with my mom in her Jeep as she approached a stop sign. She wasn't paying attention, and before the Jeep came to a rolling stop, the neighborhood crackhead appeared on a bicycle. I, too shocked to realize what was about to happen, could only whisper, "Stop," but the man catapulted in the air and back down to the concrete. I think I died for a moment because when I came back to earth, the man got back on his bike, waved and smiled at us, and carried on about his day. My mom was losing it, but about five minutes later, she realized he was OK, I was OK, and she was OK, so she proceeded to take me to school.

Ever since that day, I was afraid to ride my bike in the street. It took me many years to overcome my fear of just crossing the street on foot without being at a light. It took even longer for me to get over my fear of being behind a bike as I was driving in my car, replaying the crackhead scene over and over again in my mind. After that day, I never rode my bike again.

Until recently.

Here's how I got over that. I was on vacation in the beach city of Laguna Niguel, California, and decided it was time for a change — that what happened in my past doesn't determine my future unless I let it. Even though I was shit scared, I got on one of the resort's complimentary bikes and placed my helmet on my head full of curls. Just doing that, I felt my heart race and my panic rise. I was really going to ride a bike in the streets of LA where reckless drivers roamed. Was I to put my life in their hands? Absolutely not. I felt guided that this ride was going to be safe, and I told myself, *You are safe, you are protected, you are secure*... I repeated this mantra over and over again until my heart rate came down and I found myself ready and able to take on the ride.

Once I got going, I was OK. I stayed in the bike lane as close to the curb as possible, followed along with everyone else who was riding their bikes in the bike lane, and felt like a weight had been taken off my shoulders. My fear of riding a bike in the street was slowly fading away. *I can do this*, I said to myself. *I am doing this! I'm doing it!* I felt a smile cross my lips, and I released the fear once and for all.

Now, your fear might not be riding bikes in the street or even crossing the street for that matter, but the lesson here goes for any fear. We have to fall out with fear in order to find faith to live a fruitful life. Whenever something scary comes up, I ask myself, *What am I afraid of? What is the root of this fear?* My fear of riding a bike in the street stemmed from being in the car with my mom and seeing a man get hit while on his bike. I wasn't hit or hurt, and he was OK, but I became fearful after having a front-row experience of what could happen. But then I had to ask myself:

Is this mine?

Did I hit the man on the bike?

Did I get hurt?

The answers were no, no, and no. I had to release that fear and carry on with my life. And though the initial moments on the bike after so many years weren't fun, I took the chance and did it anyway — and I was fine. I had to fall out with my fear because that fear didn't belong to me — it was simply the result of an experience I witnessed and eventually had to let go of.

Sometimes we hang on to experiences or fears because we think we have to or because they had a profound effect on us. I had a friend once who told me she didn't drive on the highways. She only took the surface streets to get to places.

"So what if you have to go on a road trip and the highway is the only option? How do you go?"

"I don't," she said.

"Hmm. Well, why not? What happened that made you not feel safe driving on the freeway?"

She went quiet for a minute, and I realized I might have crossed a line. Maybe she wasn't ready to share with me what had happened to her, if anything at all. After a moment of silence, she sighed and opened up to me.

"People drive crazy. When I was a kid, my family and I went on a road trip, and an irate driver flipped off my dad because he was driving too slow. He followed us for miles before finally going around us, but it scared me. Ever since, I only drive the streets to avoid people like that."

"I hear you," I said. "That must have been terrifying. How old were you when it happened?"

"Oh, I think I was about fifteen or so. Right before learning how to drive was when it happened."

"Jeesh."

"Yeah, it was a scary situation to be in."

"Have you ever tried to get on the freeway and see how it feels for yourself?"

She thought about this for a minute. "I did. Once. And I enjoyed it, but I figured my luck would run out soon enough, so I never tried it again."

My friend asked me for recommendations on what she should do if she ever decided to overcome this fear of hers. Especially since she hoped one day to take her kids on road trips. She had a lot of happy memories of road trips as a kid, and she desired for her kids to have amazing experiences too. Here is a technique I gave her to help her identify if a fear even belonged to her and also to overcome her fear of the highways. I told her to ask herself the following:

- *Is this mine?* Meaning, is this fear really yours, or is it simply an outgrowth of an experience that you witnessed at some point in your life or that came from someone else? A lot of times, we pick up experiences from others and take them as our own because they've had a profound effect on us. During the road trip with her family, the irate driver didn't flip her off — it was her dad — but because that experience had a strong impact on her, she took it on as her own and translated it into a whole set of beliefs: *Drivers aren't safe. Highways aren't safe. Safety is avoiding highways. Safety is sticking to routes that are not on the highways.* If you have a fear, ask yourself this question and release this fear from your life by facing it head-on.

- *Has this happened to me?* Because she avoided the highways, she never actually dealt with a driver who was irate with her. She always drove the speed limit, and she wasn't in a rush because she always gave herself plenty of time to get to her appointments. Again, she hadn't experienced the highway driver's hostility firsthand, so she was able to release her fear because the action that triggered it hadn't happened to her. She was simply holding on to the fear instead of acknowledging it and letting it pass through her.

- *What is the worst that could happen?* She mentioned she always thought that someone would have such profound road rage toward her that they would try to attack her, and she felt fearful as a result of these thoughts. Even though she herself hadn't experienced this, she knew people who had. I asked her why she was living her life waiting for something like that to happen. If it hadn't happened to her, why was it paralyzing her from living her life? This struck a chord in her. I challenged her to take a trip on a highway, even for a few minutes, to begin the motion of taking back her power and releasing the hold that fear had over her life in this area.

Now, you may be thinking, *But what if the fear does belong to me because I did do the thing or I am guilty of what I am fearful of?* And I will tell you to face the fear and do it anyway. After I encouraged my friend to drive on the freeway, she did encounter someone who honked their horn at her for driving too slowly. Instead of tensing up as the driver drove around her, she acknowledged the fear, accepted the fear, and allowed it to pass through her. Her wife was with her and eased her anxiety by repeating the affirmations that she was safe, protected, and secure. Afterward, she pulled over into a parking lot to get herself together and then continued to drive. She realized that she could no longer live in fear of other people and that she had to take responsibility for living her best life — it wasn't going to live it for her. After a year of practicing, she finally felt confident to take her kids on a road trip. She no longer worries about irate drivers, and her fear of highways is a thing of the past.

Choosing faith over fear = a fruitful life

When we fall out of fear, we are taking our power back to live our lives. If we sit and think about what shoulda, woulda, coulda happened if we were to do the damn thing, the thing would never get done. Instead, ask yourself how silly it would be to miss out on all the opportunities you don't take. Would you rather daydream about what shoulda, woulda, coulda been? Or would you rather live in the reality of all the possibilities that can be?

I had a friend who wanted to travel the world, but whenever I asked her how her travel planning was coming, she always came up with an excuse. "Oh, you know, so many people get sick when they go to India, so I think I'm going to go to Mexico instead." I'd follow up on her trip planning to Mexico. "Oh, you know, so many Americans are getting kidnapped now in Mexico, think Imma steer clear of that one. Maybe I'll just go on a cruise instead." I'd ask about the cruise line she'd decided on. "Oh, you know, folks is getting stranded on cruise ships now, Imma just…"

I don't need to continue this story.

So anyways, back to falling out with fear.

Unlike my unnamed friend above, you have to break down and dissect what it is you're really afraid of and why. Why is she so afraid of traveling? Hell if I know, but it's probably a protection mechanism to keep herself safe and secure. Why do we sometimes feel unsafe and insecure? It could stem from something that happened to us in our childhood or as an adolescent or even as an adult. It could be from someone else's bad experience that led us to believe it could happen to us. Either way, we won't get over our fears until we face them. There are no ifs, ands, or buts about it. Once we sit down to write the damn book, we face the fear of writing a book for the masses. Once we pitch our idea to angel investors, we overcome our fear of presenting in front of others. Once we apply to the job we think we won't get anyway, we get over the fear of being rejected, because we did the work, and if they say no, it only means a better opportunity is on the way. We have to get comfortable being uncomfortable. Do you think I was cozy riding on a main road surrounded by speeding cars on a bike with a tiny seat that was so uncomfortable my thighs were sore for days *and I had no protection around my body*? No, I wasn't. I was anxious, and I felt like my heart might come out of my chest. But I did it anyway, and I lived to tell the story. I didn't sit in Shoulda, Woulda, Coulda Land coming up with make-believe stories that didn't happen. I rode the bike, and after a while, it was fun. I enjoyed it — eventually. But the main thing is that I overcame my fear. I thought it would be silly to go through life without riding a bike again, and I love riding my bike now — albeit on an enclosed trail. I had to change my perspective on my fear of riding, and once I changed my mind, I changed my reality.

I encourage you to fall the fluckity fluck out with fear. It is not your friend — it is your enabler, keeping you stuck and still in life. Below are some techniques that have helped me and countless others to fall out of fear and live amazing, fruitful lives.

- *Remember that you are always in control.* You decide if you've had enough or if you can handle a bit more. Exposing yourself to your fear bit by bit will only strengthen you. Don't overdo it either. I didn't ride my bike for fifty miles on the first try. After an hour, I had had enough. Only you will know what your limit is. Be kind to yourself and give yourself grace for facing your fear head-on.
- *Identify and change your negative thoughts about your fear.* If you're afraid of flying because you think it's dangerous, identify and challenge your belief as to why flying is danger-ous and what makes you feel it isn't safe for you. This could stem back to a negative experience, whether your own or someone else's, or just a thought pattern that you've believed to be true for you. Identifying your fears helps you to get to the root cause, which is a crucial step to overcoming them.
- *Visualize yourself actually doing whatever you're afraid of.* Maybe that's public speaking, asking someone out on a

date, running for president, climbing a mountain, being in a closed space, whatever. Just imagine yourself doing it, feeling totally relaxed, and completing it successfully. This can reduce any anxiety you may be feeling and build your confidence. Because at the end of the day, you got this!

MAGIC MOMENT

Affirmations for Kicking Fear to the Curb

Use the mantras listed below to help you fall out with fear for good.

- *I am in control of my life.*
- *I am safe, I am protected, I am secure.*
- *I choose faith over fear to live a fruitful life.*
- *What I fear is not my reality.*
- *I am bigger than my fear.*
- *I am confident and capable of overcoming any obstacle or challenge or fear.*
- *I have the inner power to overcome my fears.*
- *I am deserving of a life free of fears.*
- *I am worthy of a fear-free life.*
- *I am grateful for the opportunities to learn and grow when I face my fears.*

Conclusion

Not Even the Sky Is the Limit

The sky has no limits. Neither should you.

— Usain Bolt, aka "Lightning Bolt," Eight-Time Olympic
Gold Medal Sprinter, Eleven-Time World Champion

Being a published author has been a lifelong dream of mine. For as long as I can remember, I've had the same three goals: I wanted to get to know God on a much deeper spiritual level, travel the world, and write books for a living. Though it's taken me time to get here, I've made it, full circle, to live the life of my dreams. I say this to you because I want you to know that no matter who you are or where you live, not even the sky is the limit. You just need to believe and put in the work to get where you want to go. My life wasn't bad growing up, but I've experienced things that have changed me. It definitely has had its learning curves, and they've crafted me into the woman I am today. I share my story and those of others with you to let you know that if I can do it, so can you.

I remember when I first got the news that I'd landed a publisher for this book. I cried and told myself, *You fucking did it. You. Never. Gave. Up.* I called my mom, shared the news with her, and cried with her on the phone. I'm just a girl from Detroit, where dreams are broken because you either die before they become your reality or you're too exhausted to carry them through.

I know hard days.

I know tough times.

But I also believe in magic.

And I also believe in you.

You're reading this book because you want a way out, too. You want to live in peace and harmony and be financially abundant and have generational wealth that will pass down through the ages. You want the life you never even thought was possible for you. You want safety, security, serenity, and just to be. To sit in silence and enjoy the calmness that it brings. The reassurance of every in breath and out breath.

When I worked in HR, I used to be upset when an applicant who wasn't a person of color got a job that a person of color was overlooked for. I used to see how Black people had to work twice as hard as their non-Black counterparts simply because of the color of their skin. We all aren't angry Black women or Black men. We deserve a seat at the table too, and we don't have to work overtime to sit down. We belong here.

I used to think that the reason there are so many uneducated Black men or men who have decided to create their own futures outside of the corporate world is because they don't want to have to struggle to claim their intelligence in an environment that doesn't accept them in the first place. There are so many uneducated Black men who have been robbed of opportunities. And we see them robbing each other, killing each other because of the fed-up-ness of how unfair life can be. If only there was a glimmer of light to show them that the path doesn't have to be the one they have chosen. They don't have to choose destruction. They can choose creation.

It's true that those experiences and journeys are not my own. There are so many Black men and women who did take opportunities and have made something of themselves. But of those of us from Gladstone Street and Dexter Avenue, there are still just a few who have made it and become triumphant. We were either shot and killed or shot and lived to tell the story or know someone who was. It's either you live or you die. There is no in between. And because that was the place I grew up in, I know the harsh realities of how the world can be. Especially when you are a product of an environment you're looking for a way out of and you don't know who to turn to or what to do. Who to trust. Who's your friend? Who's your foe? You turn to God. You ask for guidance. God gives you guidance, and folks start showing up in your life. Opportunities start showing up in your life. You make good decisions. You make bad decisions. You learn. You face an obstacle. You are tested. You have a setback. You learn again. You are triumphant. *Umph.* Another setback. Another test. You learn again. And again. And again. And again. You are triumphant. And your growth is on an upward trajectory. But not without you overcoming failure upon failure upon failure along the way.

You.

Never.

Give.

Up.

You keep going because you are all you have. You depend on you. You depend on you to succeed, to overcome, to get it done. You have to. You might be tired and exhausted, but you keep on going. You are the breadwinner. You are the uplifter. The supporter. The comforter. The therapist. The coach. The momma and the daddy. The everything. You never stop. *Shoot, forgot to go to the gym today because I was up later than usual last night. Writing. No worries, I'll go harder tomorrow. Oh shoot, gotta make sure I put dinner on. What should I make? Taco Tuesday. Wash the dishes. Put the dishes away. Dry and fold the clothes.*

Clean the house. Don't forget, dinner date tomorrow with friends who just had a baby. Gotta do double duty today because I won't have time to write as much tomorrow. No worries, Imma get it done.

When you prioritize what matters the most to you, it becomes your world. Your life. Besides meeting up with friends who'd recently had a baby, I met *no one* while writing this book. I gave up my weekends for five months to *write this book*. I told my friends, "Hey guys, I love you, but this is my dream. Let's catch up in the spring." And no one objected. When you have a strong core group of friends who are your biggest cheerleaders, they will support you every step of the way. One of my closest friends waited an entire month to celebrate my birthday because I was writing my book. She even got the guys at the restaurant to sing me "Happy Birthday" as I blew out the candle on my birthday cake. *Make a wish. Dreams do come true.* And they do.

This book was written for you. For you who thought it would be impossible to follow through on your goals because procrastination had you down with its heavy hand. For you who thought that love was beyond your grasp, but now you know what to do. For you who didn't know how to make those bold dreams into your living reality. For you, trapped in a toxic relationship but now you know how to set yourself free. And for you who didn't know where to look or where to start to manifest your dream. I wrote this book for you. To help you grow, succeed, overcome, overachieve, outshine, outdo, glow up, blow up, boss up — because you deserve it. Whatever you desire to do in this world, go after it. As Jeezy sang, "The world is yours and everything in it / It's out there, get on your grind and get it." You are worthy and deserving of all the success and love and abundance you could ever wish for. It is waiting for you to claim it. Don't deny yourself the love or money or power or peace or freedom or career or family or life you want because of what somebody else thinks of you (or doesn't think of you, for that matter). This life is yours and yours alone. I can't live it for you, but you sure can. Make sure you are living your life fulfilled. You are protected, you are loved, you are safe, you are everything and more. The life you want is just waiting to be had by you. Use this book as your guide, your toolbox full of the tools you need to make it in this world and to live an amazing life. Believe in yourself and your dreams wholeheartedly, and you become an unstoppable force. Never stop dreaming or believing in yourself.

You got this!

I'm saying "Toodle-oo" here, and I wish you all the success in this world, because the world needs that special thang that only you have, and the world wouldn't be the same without your unique touch of magic.

With lots of love.

Acknowledgments

I want to thank you, my reader, for reading this book. I truly hope it helps you in some way to live your most amazing, magic-filled life. You deserve the life you want to live. You are worthy of having it, and it is waiting for you — your most Authentic Self — to come and grab it by the horns.

I want to thank my Mommi, who I love so much and who has been one of my biggest cheerleaders and supporters my whole, entire life. You never stopped believing in me, and I am proud to call you my mom. I am proud to be your daughter. Thank you for molding me into the woman I am today.

I want to thank my agent, Paul Levine, and my amazing editors, Georgia Hughes, Diana Rico, and Kristen Cashman. This work would not have been possible without your guidance, suggestions, and help in making this book the best it can be. I am grateful for you ladies — thank you so much!

To my loving and supportive husband, I love you so much! Thank you for your feedback, for challenging me to think in different perspectives and from other points of view. Your constructive feedback has made me stronger, and I love you for it.

To my friends and family in Detroit, I love you. To Candi and Dew, I love you, I love you, I love you! Thank you for being my cheerleaders. To Satara, I love you. To my family in Georgia, I love you more. To my daddy, I love and miss you every day. I hope you're proud of me. Until we meet again. To Grumma, forever in my thoughts and never forgotten, how heavy my heart still feels that you are gone. A piece of me that hasn't been replaced. I love you infinitely, and I know you're proud of me. Until next time.

To God and the Universe, thank you for pouring into me as I wrote this book. For giving me the vision to get this message out there in the world in my own unique way, in my own voice, thank you.

And last but not least, thank you to *me*. I am proud of me and the work that I have accomplished. Looking back, all I can say is, "Wow." I am beyond grateful, beyond humbled, and forever in awe of the untapped magic that I have found within myself. I have utilized it and continue to use it to the best of my ability and beyond, watching even greater manifestations come into fruition. I love you, infinitely.

XOXO,

Chloe

About the Author

Chloe Panta is a highly sought-after mindset expert and transformational coach dedicated to helping individuals achieve their ultimate life goals. With a passion for holistic coaching, she left her corporate job to pursue her dream of helping others. After working with her own techniques for several years, she established a successful coaching practice in 2017. She has been featured in numerous media outlets, including the *New York Times*, CBS, *Essence*, the *TODAY* show, *Good Morning America*, *Forbes*, *Newsweek*, and the *Los Angeles Times*, where she was praised for her insightful approach to helping clients create their ideal lives. Chloe lives in mountainous California with her husband and their dog, Bëar.

Visit Chloe's website and join her email newsletter list for updates, inspiration, and more, right in your inbox: ChloePanta.co.